# Tails of a Boarding Kennel

*P.S. This is a really cheap motel!*

Bonnie Rowley

AuthorHouse™
1663 Liberty Drive, Suite 200
Bloomington, IN 47403
www.authorhouse.com
Phone: 1-800-839-8640

First published by AuthorHouse    8/26/2008

ISBN: 978-1-4389-1404-6 (sc)

Printed in the United States of America
Bloomington, Indiana

This book is printed on acid-free paper.

authorHOUSE®

# Dedication

This book is dedicated to all who passed through our front door during the past nearly half-century and brightened the lives of three generations of pet caregivers, be they human, canine, feline, fish, fowl, or rodent. Whether they walked, crawled, bounded merrily or were dragged into our office, they all contributed in a very positive way. We offer a special thank you to the owners of these memorable creatures. We are eternally grateful that you have entrusted us with your extended family. This book represents your gift to us.

## Prologue

## The Why's and Wherefores of These Tails

A little explanation is in order as to why I would put all of these stories, poems, and thoughts into book form.  My family began a boarding kennel in 1963.  This came after spending years boarding the dogs that they took to Dog Shows, breeding dogs, and just generally being in the "Dog Business".  We purchased our first show dog, a collie by the name of Bruce, when I was a mere five years old.

So I suppose it's safe to say that I grew up in a total dog environment, not to mention cats, birds, ducks, fish, hamsters, mice, bunnies, and horses.  All of our pets co-habitated nicely and only on rare occasions were there any clashes.

Upon my parent's retirement, my husband Ed and I purchased the kennel.  Each decade brought more additions and improvements, until the original 50 dog kennel grew to over 200.  Today, our son Todd owns it, since we've retired as well.  The kennel continues to flourish, with the addition of Pet Suites, and even more pens.  We've actually had customers who have boarded with us through three generations. It is gratifying to have developed trust that continues on after all of these years.

Since our retirement, I've collected all sorts of memorabilia, which has been patiently awaiting organization.  Behind this always lurked the thought of sharing my stories with other dog lovers.  Some of these memories are stored "in my head", and like my computer, memory is beginning to be limited with age.  The time has come to write these stories, sort of run a back-up hard copy, before they are lost forever.  Some of these pets truly need to be immortalized somehow.

As far as who this book is geared to, there are two answers.  Of course, it's for people who love dogs and cats, but a deeper target is
> A) People who have boarded their pets, and maybe felt a little guilty about it.
> B)  People who have never "had to board" their pets, and are proud of it.

For the "A" people, I hope to reassure them that they have, indeed, shared their pets with people who have grown to love them like family.  That sometimes the best thing you can do for a pet is to cave in to that pack mentality and allow them to be around others of their kind.  And that loving your pet does not mean isolating him from humanity and canine companionship.

For the "B" people, I hope to dispel the attitude that boarding is a jail sentence, and the pens are like "death row".  This attitude can be relayed to your dog when you leave him, and because our pets are so in tune with our feelings and moods, they may, by osmosis, develop the same fear.  Please don't wait until your pet is old and decrepit to leave him.  That is like taking Grandma from the nursing home to Grand Central Station! Introduce him to the fun side of boarding while he is still a pup and believes everyone, four legged and two legged, loves him.  They will.

So much for the soapbox.  The main reason for this little book is that I just plain wanted to write it for the fun of it.  After all, isn't that the best part of having a pet -fun?

Many of the dogs pictured here don't have a story attached.  That doesn't mean they weren't worthy of one, only that their personalities were just plain sweet.  Just because they weren't quirky doesn't mean we didn't love them.  They simply never did anything out of the ordinary-they were just lovable pooches.  They are the kind that will always be a kennel owner's dream.  And how could anyone complain about that?  Also, when pictures were unavailable, I used ones that were a close representation of the story.  Apologies to the stars for the use of stand-ins.

Fittingly, the introduction to this book begins with one of the many letters and postcards we've received throughout the years; or should I say our guests have received, since that's really who they were intended for.  Just to keep the record straight, each of these was delivered to, sniffed by, and read to the appropriate dog. (Not necessarily the cats, as they couldn't care less!)  By doing so, I quelled my conscience into thinking it was permissible to then keep them to share one day in a book.  After all, usually the dogs ate them anyway!

At any rate, I wish to thank little Jenny for the use of her PPSS. in the title.  Its things like this that made our Dog Daze so memorable.

Dear Ruffles,

I Really miss you! We just came to Kirksville to check out Dads Radio station Now Mon. Tue we will be in town and on wed. We leave for cal. We will be gone 2 weeks Well be back July 4 but its holiday so we will pick you On the 6. I am going to send you about 3 more postcards

I LOVE you,

Your sister,
Jennifer

PS.
I only wish you could read

P.P ss

This is a really cheap motel.

"I know that dogs are pack animals, but it's difficult to imagine a pack of standard poodles...and if there was such a thing as a pack of standard poodles, where would they rove to? Bloomingdale's?"

Yvonne Clifford

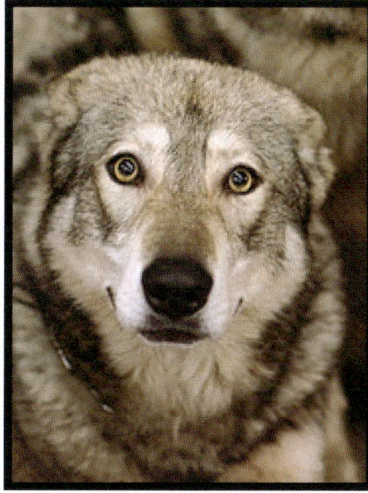

*"I've seen a look in dogs' eyes, a quickly vanishing look of amazed contempt, and I am convinced that basically dogs think humans are nuts."*

*John Steinbeck*

Captain Nemo

Not all of our guests were sweet, cuddly, and good-natured. Some of them were just plain cantankerous and grouchy, with a mile-long mean streak. As strange as it may sound, that is precisely what made them so endearing. Sweet can get boring after a while. With this in mind, you may try to comprehend why Captain Nemo was one of our favorites through two generations of boarding.

Nemo was a stocky little West Highland White Terrier, or Westie for short, and an office mascot. Since his owner was also the owner of the company, Nemo did pretty much what Nemo wanted at work, much to the dismay of the employees. Being bit by Captain Nemo was pretty much an occupational hazard. He went to work Monday through Friday, however for many years he wasn't allowed in the family home. I suppose that's because the Mrs. and Nems had a mutual distain for one another. Therefore, every Friday evening until Monday morning, we were Nemo's home away from home (or office).

To an uninformed observant, it may have sounded like an exile, but to Nems it was just an extension of places to show his authority. In he would come, swagger actually, and beware of anything that would get in his way. Lines were for peons, so he would naturally go to the front. Since he would bite anyone else that was in the office, this was permissible.

All the dogs were given a quick physical upon arrival, and Nemo would tolerate this, if only one person (who wasn't afraid of him) would do it. If in a semi-good mood, you could get away with the check-in without too many tribulations. If in a foul mood, however, his ears would be laid back on his head, like a very unhappy donkey, and it was best to use the only bribe that ever worked: Velveeta cheese.

We always gave out the medications in Velveeta, so it was readily (thank goodness!) available; a fact Nemo knew only too well. If you looked him straight in the eye and said, "If you behave, I'll get you some cheese" he would tolerate most anything, including a bath and brushing. But Nemo had the memory of an elephant, so if you ever reneged on the cheese, he would make you pay dearly!

Nemo loved to intimidate the other dogs. At the time, there were metal partitions between the pens, and he would take his paw and pound on it, then peek under the pen to make certain the dog next door was duly intimidated. For this reason, he was usually in an end pen, or next to some equally fearless creature.

Another of his tricks was to get his five-gallon stainless steel water bowl out of the ring that held it, and use it to smack around the pen, like a hockey puck. There were countless dented bowls, until we finally learned to put his food and water in a metal bucket, and clip it to the gate. We always tried to inform new kennel help about Nemo's quirks, but invariably they would forget and put a bowl in his pen. Releasing him into the outside pen didn't help, as he would just take the bowl with him and continue the hockey game outside. Once the newcomers were initiated by having to retrieve the bowl, they rarely made that same mistake again.

Nemo was also co-pilot of the company airplane. We all could clearly imagine him in the seat next to his owner, with a hand-crocheted scarf around his neck, looking every bit like the original Red Baron.

Captain Nemo, in his travels, was the proud owner of a beautiful leather collar from Switzerland. It contained a little snap pocket, in which was placed a quarter. This was for calling home if things weren't just as Nemo liked them. We are proud to say that not once in all of those years did he ever have to make that telephone call.

"The dog was created specially for children.
He is the god of frolic."

Henry Ward Beecher

Buddy

Once upon a time, a lovely elderly couple toured the kennel. They were very impressed, and made a reservation for their shepherd mix named Buddy. When the day arrived to check in Buddy, we quickly realized this was no one's buddy, except for maybe the owners. And even that was "iffy".

Buddy was a big boy, nearly 90 pounds of muscle. He had short hair, German Shepherd markings, and somewhat of a sweet face…until he let out a noise that made the hairs on the nape of your neck stand on end. Never in the history of the kennel had any of us experienced such a growl! The sound began very low, as if from the pits of hell. As we were checking him in, which required going through his coat, checking his feet, ears, etc. the hair on his back stood straight up, from the tip of his nose to his tail. The growl slowly increased in volume, until it became fever pitch.

His owners kept assuring us what a sweet dog he was, but ever fiber of our being screamed "Be Careful!" True to his growl, not his owner's beliefs, this was one nasty critter. We tried putting him in a section of the kennel that wasn't being used, so he would stay calm and hopefully mellow a bit. When we would open the door to that section, before you could even turn on the lights, you could hear his growl reverberating off the walls. The feeling was that of walking into a lion's den.

Good old Buddy figured out that if he didn't go outside when it was time for exercise, we would have to go into his pen and take him out, as the pen had to be cleaned. This gave him the golden opportunity to attempt to kill the person cleaning the pen. We finally figured out the only way to get him to go outside was to use human "bait". Someone (once making sure their life insurance was paid up) would go into the outside pen and call him, while the person inside would hold open the guillotine door. He would make a lunge for the meal on legs outside, and we would slam the door shut and clean the pen. Then, reverse the situation to get him to come back inside.

The couple were such nice people, my husband Ed just couldn't tell them what a miserable animal they owned and just kept taking Dear Old Buddy. That is, until the entire staff rebelled and convinced him someone was going to become dinner, and it wasn't going to be the puppy chow. We never heard where they left Buddy after he was expelled from Williamsburg, but chances are there became a few less kennel staff somewhere in St. Louis.

"I think we are drawn to dogs because they are the uninhibited creatures we might be if we weren't certain we knew better."

George Bird Evans

**Dirty & Rude**

*"They (dogs) never talk about themselves but listen to you while you talk about yourself, and keep up an appearance of being interested in the conversation."*

*Jerome K. Jerome*

Bubba & Puppy

When I hear people who are concerned about leaving their animals in a kennel for an extended period of time, it always brings to mind Bubba and Puppy, who tie for the longest stay at our kennel.

Their owner was getting married to a gentleman with children. This is a common occurrence these days, but there was a complication that proved to be quite a challenge to the relationship. The children (his) were allergic to the dogs (hers). After some serious discussion, some ground rules were established: If the kids were staying, so were the dogs. At this point, a contractor was hired to build a house that was quite custom: one wing for the kids and one for the dogs. If the kids weren't going to live in the garage or basement, neither were the dogs. Both being of utmost importance in the family scheme, both were to made to feel as welcome as possible.

Of course, the normal time between hiring an architect and the actual completion of the house was one year. Bubba and Puppy had a good Mom. She came several times per week to take them for walks or go into the back yard for a little bonding. When she would overhear another client saying how badly they felt leaving their pets so long, she would make sure the concerned client knew that her family was there for a year, and look how happy her dogs were!

It's only natural to become quite attached to pets that you spend so much time with. Bubba and Puppy were two of the cutest little mix breeds you could imagine, both shaggy, one gray and one black. If you could manage to clone them, they would surely become one of the most popular breeds offered by the AKC.

At the end of their stay, Bubba and Puppy had a happy reunion with their real family, and a tearful goodbye with their Williamsburg family. We couldn't help but wonder if the children faired as well during their year. As a going away present, we were presented with an ornament for the Christmas tree that looked for the world like Bubba. The owners tried to find one that looked like Puppy, too, but with no success. To this day, when I hang that ornament on the tree, I think of these wonderful dogs and the special family to which they belong.

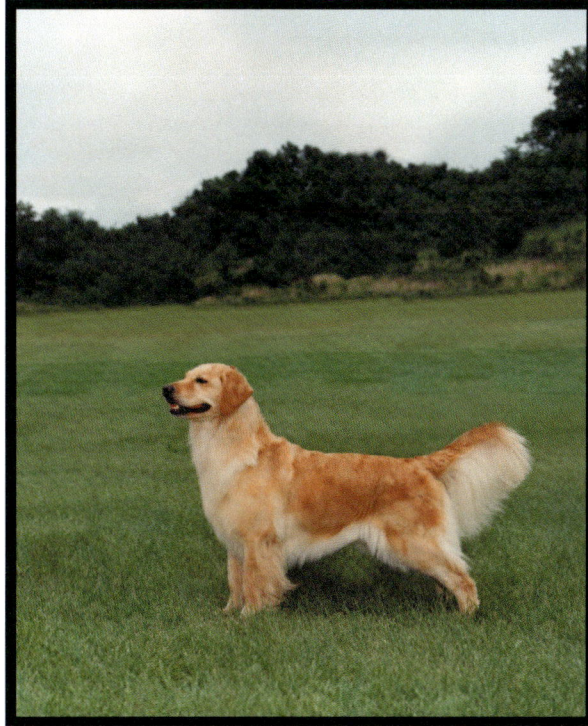

Ch. Molega's One of a Kind (Solo)

*"If you pick up a starving dog and make him prosperous, he will not bite you; that is the principal difference between a dog and a man."*

*Mark Twain*

Beau

Among the exotics we boarded was a Parrot named Beau. Beau was an African Grey, and at the time we were not set up for aviary boarding. Beau's owners, however, had cats and dogs, and just didn't want to take Beau to a different facility. After much cajoling, they convinced us to take Beau.

Being a fairly young pubescent African Grey, he was just entering his "talking stage" and had yet to utter a word. We spoke to him constantly, in the hope that we could encourage him to say something prolific and surprise his owners when it was time to go home.

The only location we had to place his cage was in the feeding room, where food preparation takes place three times per day. We thought it was a good place, as he would have lots of company, and it was far from the chaos of the kennel, and God forbid, the cattery. There was one flaw in our thinking.

This was prior to the development of pagers for the employees, so when someone was needed in the office to check in or retrieve a pet, we would ring an electric bell-type buzzer to summon the staff. One bell was in the food room, and another in the kennel proper.

Much to everyone's dismay, Beau's first sound was a resounding BUZZZ! He would ruffle his feathers, lower his head, and let lose with a buzz that would put any chain saw to shame. This, soon to be followed with a barking that sounded for the world like an angry Rottweiler! We were immensely grateful that Beau's owners had a sense of humor when they came to pick him up. They said if their dogs didn't scare a burglar away, their parrot would!

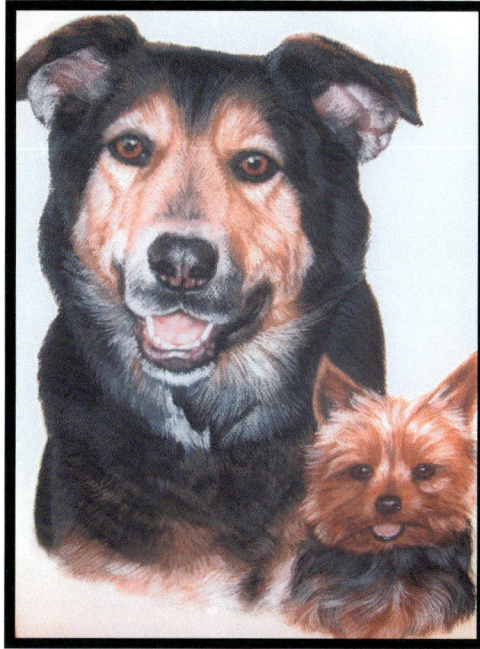

**Winfield & Reebok**

Of the many animals who have endeared themselves to our family throughout those Dog Daze, none have captured our hearts more than Winfield and Reebok.

My Grandmother found it necessary to move into a nursing home in the late 80's. We were very fortunate to find Surrey Place, owned by St. Luke's Hospital here in St. Louis. Surrey Place was a very open minded and progressive Home, run by a director who always put her patient's well-being above protocol. When one of the Security Guards showed up with a puppy, who had been abandoned, Kim decided a live-in pet for the residents was not only do-able, but just the thing they needed.

Spending a great deal of my time at Surrey Place, and being dog-oriented, I had my concerns. In no way did I feel this was any less than a wonderful idea, but the pup was obviously a German Shepherd mix, not always known for their pleasant temperament. Also, his size was an issue. I would flinch when I saw Winfield galloping down the hall, in pure, disjointed, puppy fashion. While the residents in the halls would be tottering along on walkers, or shuffling down the hall holding guard rails, along would bound this gangly, long-legged pup. Eventually I stopped cringing, when it became apparent that Winfield had total control where his Senior Friends were concerned. He would come to a screeching halt in front of them, and sit patiently awaiting a pat on the head.

Our Veterinarian, Caroline Truss, had concerns, too. She volunteered to take care of Winfield medically at no charge, and offered advice on do's and don'ts of having a resident animal. Kim welcomed the input, as she hoped the situation would be beneficial to all involved. While visiting animals, like Pet Partners, are welcomed by the populace, there simply is no comparison to having a pet to call one's own.

Winfield became the best ice-breaker at Surrey Place.  When visitors would enter the living room, residents would be sitting around not speaking with one another.  Enter: Winfield.  Everyone in the room would vie for his attention.  Dutifully, he would make the rounds, so as not to show favorites.  Even when he wasn't in evidence, someone would bring him up, and discussions would take place about all of the endearing things their dog did that day.

One of Dr. Truss' concerns was aggression.  She was worried that someone would run over his tail with a wheel chair, or have a seizure while holding his ear, or some other unintentional harm that may befall our pup.  No matter how accidental, he simply could not show hostility.   Because of this, she suggested I take a bone, or other delectable item, and give it to him.  Then I was to pry his  mouth open, and take it away again.  While I felt like I was being cruel, he seemed to take it all in his stride.   He passed each and every test with flying colors.

Kim and I spoke frequently about Winfield's impact on the people of Surrey Place. The staff loved him as much as their charges, and he was like a permanent fixture in the building.  When someone would come through the front door, if he didn't appear right away their first question was "Where's Winfield?"  With this, the receptionist would get on the PA and say, "Would Sir Winfield report to the reception area, please?"  Within a minute or two, out would bound the Official Greeter.

The sad part of the story was that most dogs have one or two owners, and when they pass away the pets are grief-stricken.  Winfield had over 200 owners, and since it was a Nursing Home, death was not uncommon.  Kim said Winfield would lie in front of the door of a newly deceased resident and whine for days.

On the other hand, he brought so much comfort to others.  As if God placed him on this Earth for no other reason, he seemed to know just what to do when others were grieving.  A doctor, whose wife had an inoperable tumor, never would allow his feelings to surface in front of the nurses at the home. All knew she was dying, and thought it would benefit the doctor to receive some compassion from the staff, but he remained steadfastly stoic.  When her time finally came, her husband arrived and went into the room to be with her at the end.  Kim, being concerned for the doctor, peeked into the cracked door of her room.  His wife had passed on; the doctor was holding onto Winfield and sobbing.  Although he hadn't paid any attention to Winfield previously, the dog instinctively knew when to be available.  From that time on, no one ever saw the doctor again, but a huge box of Milkbones arrived each Christmas for Winfield.

At one point, someone started a rumor that St. Luke's Hospital Director was unhappy about dog food being one of the items budgeted for Surrey Place. This began an all-out rebellion by the residents and their families. Letters began to pour into St. Luke's declaring overwhelming support for Winfield. Very soon a letter came to everyone from the director declaring this was all a huge mistake. He was in total agreement as to the importance of the resident animal, and Winfield was to continue to call Surrey Place home for the rest of his days.

**Marie Lundgren & Winfield**
**1990**

A few years after Winnie had established himself as the most popular creature at Surrey, Kim decided to add another dog. While Winfield was tolerant of families bringing their pets into visit "his" people, you could tell he wanted them to know that this was, in fact, his house they were visiting. They could come, but eventually they must also go. Well, when Reebok, a four pound Yorkshire terrier, showed up and decided to make Surrey his home as well, Winfield just sighed, and as usual, adjusted.

Unlike Winfield, now sedate in his middle age, Reebok was a bundle of energy. He chased balls endlessly, but had ADD and just couldn't seem to sit still long enough to be petted. The combination of dog personalities was a constant source of entertainment for the staff, residents, and guests. When Reebok would get too annoying to deal with any longer, Winnie would simply put Reebok's entire upper torso into his mouth and contain him until he settled down a bit.

Despite his hyper ways, Reebok also developed that sixth sense that told him when to be serious. When we had to break the news of my sister Kathi's death to my Grandmother, Winfield sat right next to her wheel chair, and Reebok curled up on her lap for an endless amount of time while she cried. They both had a Ph.D in Grief Counseling.

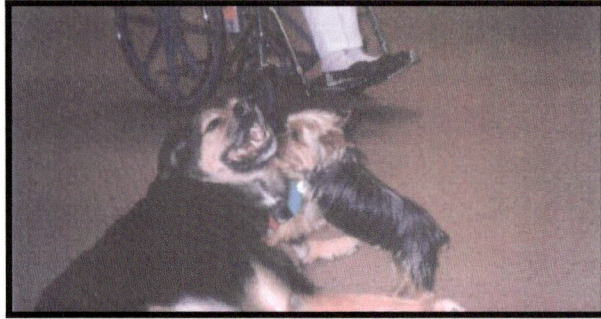

In spite of all his smarts, Winfield was a sucker for food. And the patients were suckers for saving it for him. In spite of repeated talks from Dr. Truss, at which they would all nod in understanding while she explained that this was unhealthy, each and every one fed him. Now, when more than two hundred people feed a dog, there is going to be a problem. Winfield should have weighed about sixty pounds, but actually tipped the scales at around eighty! I used to watch at meal times, while widows and widowers scooped their half-eaten dinner into bags and purses. The thought of a muzzle would have created havoc, so the staff just did the best they could to discourage this practice. His big, soulful eyes were his downfall. My Grandmother used to say, "See, he just looks hungry". Diets really are the pits!

These two delightful pups stayed with us at the kennel on a few occasions, but most of the time they had more caretakers than any two canines I know. When they finally grew too old to handle all the stress of taking care of their people, they retired to live with Kim until God, I'm sure, found a special place in heaven for Surrey Place's two Angels.

Reebok

Winfield

*"In order to keep a true perspective of one's importance, everyone should have a dog that will worship him and a cat that will ignore him."*

*Dereke Bruce*
*Taipei, Taiwan*

"In order to really enjoy a dog, one doesn't merely try to train him to be semi human.  The point of it is to open oneself to the possibility of becoming partly a dog."

Edward Hoagland

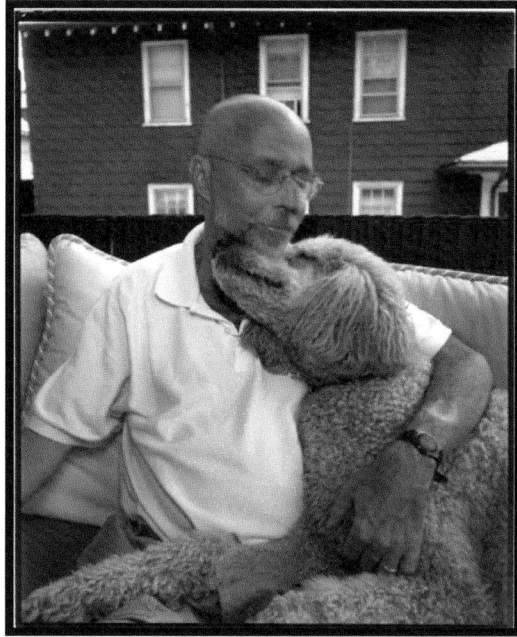

*"He is my other eyes that can see above the clouds; my other ears that hear above the winds. He is the part of me that can reach out into the sea. He has told me a thousand times over that I am his reason for being: by the way he rests against my leg; by the way he thumps his tail at my smallest smile; by the way he shows his hurt when I leave without taking him. (I think it makes him sick with worry when he is not along to care for me.) When I am wrong, he is delighted to forgive. When I am angry, he clowns to make me smile. When I am happy, he is joy unbounded. When I am a fool, he ignores it. When I succeed, he brags. Without him, I am only another man. With him, I am all-powerful. He is loyalty itself. He has taught me the meaning of devotion. With him, I know a secret comfort and a private peace. He has brought me understanding where before I was ignorant. His head on my knee can heal human hurts. His presence by my side is protection against my fears of dark and unknown things. He has promised to wait for me...whenever...wherever – in case I need him. And I expect I will – as I always have. He is just my dog."* - Gene Hill

Chel

Basset Hounds have never been known for their vivaciousness. They actually only have two speeds…High and Off. They are the epitome of "laid back". If the breed were a day of the week, it would definitely be Sunday.

One of our favorite Basset Hounds was a male named Chel (pronounced: Shell). I regret never having asked his owner how he came by that name, but Chel it was. Even in the world of the Basset, Chel was slow, with a capital S. It took him what seemed like hours to navigate from the office to the grooming room, where he crashed after being plum tuckered out from the effort.

Chel's owner loved clean dogs, and always requested a bath prior to leaving the kennel. This was quite a process, as he was much too heavy to carry to the grooming area. We usually had enough foresight to keep him in a pen close the the tub, since waiting for him to walk the length of the kennel was painstakingly slow.

Once in the tub, Chel would begin to "shrink" even as the shampoo was being applied. He just was much too tired to stand in the tub for an entire bath without a nap. His feet would begin to slide outward, and he would continue getting shorter and shorter until he was lying, spread eagle fashion, in the bottom of the tub. His ears would be splayed out to the side like wings, and he would begin to snore.

While many dogs were a challenge to keep in the tub while bathing, everyone wanted to bath Chel, as the only challenge was to carry him to the drying crate without interrupting his dreams of, what else…a cat nap!

"Dogs love their friends and bite their enemies, quite unlike people, who are incapable of pure love and always have to mix love and hate in their object-relations."

Sigmund Freud

*"In dog training, jerk is a noun, not a verb."*

Dr. Dennis Fetko

Cindy & Lady

Two of the cutest and most personable pups to ever grace our kennel were littermate Cairn Terriers. They were naturally blonde but far from stupid. Their owners had two equally adorable twin daughters, hence the twin Cairns.

Cindy and Lady loved to come to the kennel. Their favorite game while visiting was "rob your neighbor". At the time, prior to the latest remodeling, there was about an inch under the partition separating the pens. This was for cleaning purposes, and rarely caused a problem, except for the errant Nylabone that slid from one pen to another.

It did, however, pose a big problem while Cindy and Lady were in attendance. Their quest for the entire stay was to steal anything and everything from their neighbors on both sides. We usually put them in an end pen, so as to minimize their neighbors to one, and that was enough to keep the staff busy most of the day.

Depending on the item to be stolen, it may take them the better part of the day to work it under the partition. We always allowed the pets to have whatever their owners brought from home, as we felt it gave them a sense of security to have familiar things in their temporary homes. Some of these items were a bit unwieldy, but as long as the pet had room to move around we would allow it in with them.

Cindy and Lady never stole from necessity. They, too, had beds, toys, etc. in their pen. It was just the game they enjoyed. We witnessed them pulling an entire queen sized comforter into their pen, while the little dog next door watched in dismay. We would go in to retrieve it, and 10 minutes later a quarter of it would be back in their pen.

When picking up her dogs one day, the owner had a question. She said, "Now, this isn't a complaint, but we were just wondering why Cindy and Lady's noses are always raw when we pick them up". I then asked her to follow me into the kennel. As we peeked around into their pen, there they were, in the middle of a robbery. Their little tails were in the air wagging like mad, noses on the ground, tugging away. The owner laughed hysterically, and said, "Well, that explains that!" She decided they were having much too much fun to isolate them just to protect their noses, so they continued to have fun with us, and us with them, for the rest of their days.

*Sandy*

*"You can say any foolish thing to a dog, and the dog will give you a look that says, 'Wow, you're right! I never would have thought of that!'"*

*Dave Barry*

*"Children and dogs are as necessary to the welfare of the country as Wall Street and the railroads."*

*Harry S. Truman*

**Franzie**

When I was growing up, I never remember a time without pets, and always at least one dog was among them. A Doberman named Franzie was my best buddy during grade school.

Franzie was Army trained, and (we were told) would attack on command. We never really needed to use the words, "Give 'em Hell". Usually just his presence was enough to make everyone mind their P's and Q's. When put "on guard", he would patrol the house, checking every window and door.

The irony of this is that when "off guard" Franzie carried a rag doll, known as Baby. He never went anywhere without Baby, even in the yard to do his business. When sleeping, Baby was always tucked between his huge paws, and he would rest his head on it like any doting parent.

My Grandmother took me on vacations each summer, and part of the tradition was to find a new Baby for Franzie. The old ones wore out at a rapid rate, what with all the drooling and trips to the yard. He would literally act like a kid with a new toy when we would present his souvenir.

One day while taking Franzie for a walk, we had a terrible misunderstanding with a little girl walking her doll in a doll buggy. As we passed her, Franzie took one look at the doll, which resembled one of his, and snatched it right out of the buggy! Of course, the little girl began to scream, and people came running from their houses, afraid that the huge attack dog had harmed the child. Even after all discovered what the fuss was about, it took a while to convince Franzie to let go of the doll. I actually had to go home and get his before he would believe that the girl hadn't stolen his Baby!

One of our other pets that shared the house with Franzie was a tiny yellow parakeet named Tweetie, who for some reason, didn't like dogs…or maybe it was just Franzie. I can't even blame the proverbial "pecking order", as Tweetie came second.

We would allow Tweetie some time each day out of his cage for exercise and a little bonding. He would bond with us just fine, but not Franzie. In fact, the little fella had a mean streak. He thought it was hysterical to "dive bomb" the dog. Leaving from the height of the drapery rod, he would fly down, peck Franzie on the back of the head, and then retreat to his cage. You could almost see the little instigator chuckling, proud as punch that he could take advantage of something 100 times his size.

While Franzie was one of the gentlest giants on the face of the earth, even he had his limits. Finally, he reached the last straw on the camel's back, or in this case, the last bird on the dog's back. As Tweetie was zeroing in for the attack, Franzie just reached up, opened his huge mouth, and literally plucked Tweetie out of mid-air. He didn't harm a feather on his head, but laid him gently down on the carpet in front of his paws and watched him.

Tweetie's heart was pounding so hard we could see it from across the room. After a few minutes he shook off the dog slobber, and made his unsteady flight back to his cage.

Okay, so they never became friends, but they certainly reached a mutual understanding. Tweetie never even dreamed of flying near the dog again.

*"There is no psychiatrist in the world like a puppy licking your face."*

*Ben Williams*

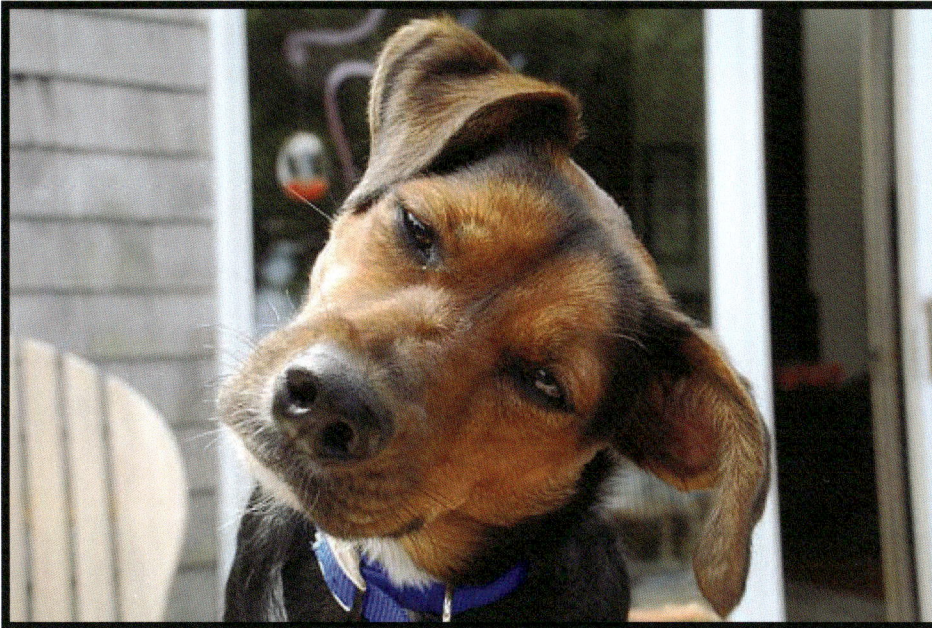

"You may have a dog that won't sit up, roll over or
even cook breakfast, not because she's too stupid to learn how
but because she's too smart to bother."

Rick Horowitz
Chicago Tribune

**Friday**

Some dogs are spineless. No, I don't mean they're not brave. I mean they can fold into an object that is nearly impossible to get a handle on. Even with many, many years experience in dealing with dogs, these specific types are a huge challenge. Big dogs, strong dogs, even aggressive dogs do not begin to present the problem of the spineless dogs.

Friday was one such animal. She was a tiny mite, probably eight pounds soaking wet. She had tall ears, short legs, a relatively long body, and like Gucci, she was an original. Our best guess would be that she was part Doxie, but a Greyhound had to have been in her ancestry somewhere.

Her owners had taken her to half the kennels in town, only to receive a phone call that she had tried to escape, and was not welcome back to their facility. After some assurance that we boarded another dog, Houdini, with the same reputation, Friday's owners decided to entrust her to us.

Our kennel has at least three sets of doors between the dog pens and the office, and yet another between there and the outside world. After the first day, it became apparent that Friday was hell-bent on traversing all of them.

Many times a day, a kennel attendant is in and out of all of the dog pens. Once or twice to put in the food bowls, and refill the water, at least once to clean, and many more times to give attention to the pets. Also, if a dog won't go outside for the exercise every few hours, one must "encourage" the guest to go outside to do his or her duty. This also applies to dogs that won't come back in without coaxing.

Friday figured out quickly that if she didn't go out, or come in from her outside pen, someone would open the gate. Once the door was opened, Friday would become "spineless". She would sprint through the open door, and no one, regardless of experience, could stop her. You would swear the dog had no bones what-so-ever!

Friday boarded with us for many years, and she realized early on that she really couldn't escape, but that didn't take away the fun of trying. We always warned the new help, as if they actually could do anything about it. You could just count on Friday, streaking up the aisle, her little legs going like wheels, ears flying in the breeze, until she had to come to a screeching halt at the next door. And there she stood, all but smiling, awaiting someone to take her back to her pen.

It was all a part of the game, and we all enjoyed it every bit as much as Friday did.

*"If dogs could talk it would take a lot of the fun out of owning one."*

Andy Rooney

**Cayman**

**The Life of a Puppy**

This morning I woke up & kissed my dad's head,
I peed on the carpet, then went back to bed.
"The life of a puppy, oh my, this is great."
Then I thought about breakfast, "I hope it's not late."

Mom took me outside, we walked for a while.
This never fails to make Mama smile.
I sniffed of everything that we did pass,
I ate something weird – it gave me gas.

I'm sure God loves me, I know that is true.
He gave me so many great things to chew.
Rugs, plants or rocks, I really don't care.
What I truly like best is Dad's underwear.

That obedience book was sort of yummy.
Though it didn't sit well on my poor puppy tummy.
I threw up a bit, but that was all right,
When Mom found it later, I was well out of sight.

I made streamers of T.P. while running at full speed.
Mom is pretty quick – but I was still in the lead.
I flew under the bed, and Mom flew past,
She stopped – shook her head, and breathed, "You're just too fast!"

Mama later phoned Daddy, and said, "it was frightening!"
That afternoon, she was sure I'd pooped lightening.
She sat at the computer, while I chewed the cord,
She thought I was mad, but I was just bored.

When Mama had enough, couldn't take anymore,
That's when my tushy got shoved out the door.
I love it inside, but outside is best.
Lay in the cool grass, and had a good rest.

That didn't last long, there was too much to do –
Can't quite remember where I hid Daddy's shoe.
I found an old bone, and scratched at a flea,
I watched the dumb squirrels as they jumped in a tree.

I barked at the kids, when they got off the bus.
I can't figure out why this makes Mama fuss.
I barked at the neighbor, I barked at the wind.
I barked and barked, 'till Mom yelled, "Come in."

The sun dipped in the west – soon Daddy would come!
I sure love my daddy: we always have fun.
I barked at my daddy, then turned on my charms,
I woo-wooed, "Hello," then jumped in his arms.

Sitting under the table – it's sooo hard to wait.
Daddy slipped me a goodie right off his plate.
I raced through the house, and scattered my toys,
Ricocheted off the furniture, and made lots of noise.

Mom found her purse – the one I abused.
Daddy let loose a chuckle.  Mom asked "Amused??"
I cowered down low, I must be in trouble.
Dad said, "Wasn't MY boy, it must be his double!"

Mom turned off the TV, and said, "Time for bed."
Dad said "Let's go boy," and patted my head.
I got in my spot, between Mom and Dad,
I thought 'bout my day and what fun I had.

Mama kicked out my bone from the covers below,
Then let loose a sigh – a sigh deep and low.
She gave me a kiss, and snuggled me tight,
And whispered so softly, "My darling, goodnight."

Unknown

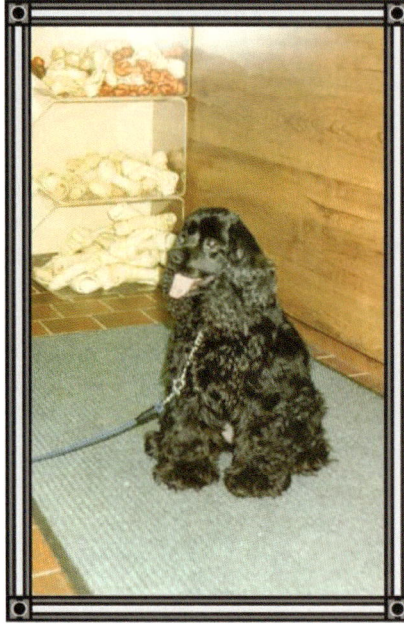

**Dutchess**

## When I Get My New Dog

I asked for strength that I might rear her perfectly;
I was given weakness that I might feed her more treats.

I asked for good health that I might rest easy;
I was given a "special needs" dog that I might know nurturing.

I asked for an obedient dog that I might feel proud;
I was given stubbornness that I might feel humble.

I asked for compliance that I might feel masterful;
I was given a clown that I might laugh.

I asked for a companion that I might not feel lonely;
I was given a best friend that I would feel loved.

I got nothing I asked for,
But everything that I needed.

Unknown

**Max**

Advertising is important in small business.  One of the best forms of publicity is location.  Residing on one of the busiest streets in the area was, without a doubt, our best form of advertising.  "Location, location, location," as they say.

Our second best form of publicity was a Golden Retriever named Max, who lived a mile or so from the kennel, and legitimately boarded with us frequently.  It was the illegitimate times that were our best advertising.

Being a member of a breed known for their wandering nature, as well as their need for constant attention and companionship, Max became easily bored at home when the kids were in school.  Despite every attempt by his owners, the minute nothing of interest was occurring, Max would jump the fence and head over to his friends at Williamsburg.  He had to cross a couple of minor streets, a small pond, a school and a McDonald's, but he would show up at our office door at least once a month.

Often a customer would come to pick up their pet and be greeted by Max, standing by the office door.  When the person opened the door and came in, Max was at their side.  The secretary would ask who this was, and the client would say "I have no idea!"  We would then take a closer look and realize it was Max.  He would run into the grooming room, and roll over waiting to be checked for fleas and ticks which he invariably had, after the pond swim.

After dipping him for "critters" we would call Max's Mom and say it was Williamsburg. She would say, "Oh, no, not again!"  She said she often felt embarrassed by his frequent return to the kennel.  "We DO give him attention, honestly" she would assure us.

Max was even keenly aware of our office hours.  If he arrived after 6 p.m. he knew the office was closed, so he would come to the front door.  The local paper did a story about Max, and many of our customers were aware of the situation.  He was their assurance that the kennel was truly a fun place to be, and they shouldn't feel guilty leaving their pet with us.  As far as payola goes, the only thing Max ever received was Milk Bones and hugs, but we received advertising that money couldn't possibly buy.  Thanks again, Max!

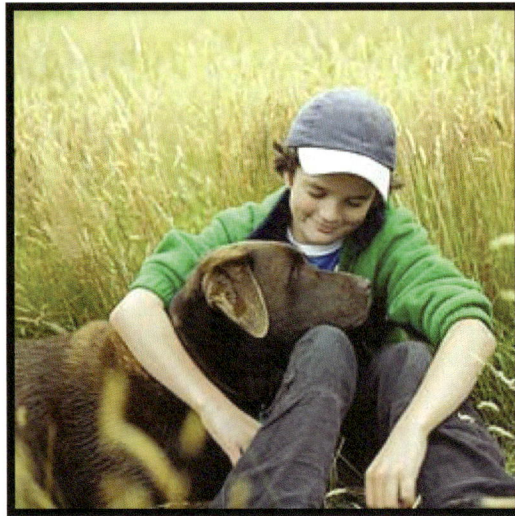

"Dogs are our link to paradise.
 They don't know evil or jealousy or discontent.
To sit with a dog on a hillside on a glorious afternoon is to
be back in Eden, where doing nothing was not boring - it
was peace."

Milan Kundera

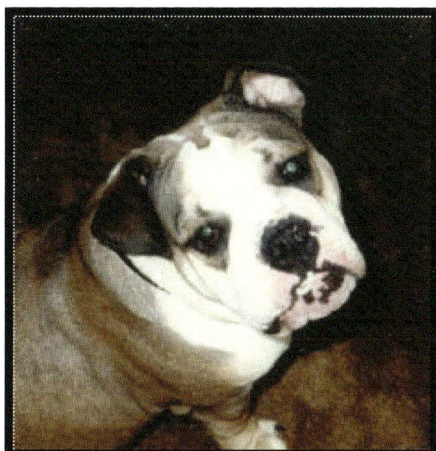

**Gus**

There has always been much speculation regarding the similar appearance of pet and owner. In most cases, there is little connection, but in a rare few, the resemblance is striking.

As previously mentioned, we boarded many sports celebrity's dogs. One of the most memorable was a Cardinal football player named Terry Stieve, and his two English Bulldogs, named Gus and Stud.

When Mr. Stieve would come in to drop them off, the likeness was unmistakable. All three had necks that were the size of the average mans waist. As they would lumber into the office, there would be little room for any other customers.

Gus and Stud seemed to enjoy their stays at Williamsburg, however in typical Bulldog fashion, they had little urge to go out and run around barking at all of the other dogs. In fact, when the kennel was exercised it became quite a challenge to get either one, let alone both, outside. Sometimes we would give in, but when the pen needed its daily cleaning, it just wasn't an option to clean around them. Two Bulldogs in the same pen gives one very little room to clean. So, we would position ourselves behind them, foot under their bottom, hands on their shoulders, and say, "Okay, Boys, it's time to go outside." With this, we would push with all our might. It was like moving two miniature mountains! After about ten minutes of this, it would be apparent the Boys were going nowhere! They would simply glance over their massive shoulders with a look that clearly said, "What on earth do you think you're doing back there?"

We would then have to get a lead, and take each for a walk around the building while the pen was cleaned. We were never certain just how much exercise Gus and Stud had received, but the staff had one heck of a workout during their stays!

Lucia

*"I wonder if other dogs think poodles are members of a weird religious cult."*

*Rita Rudner*

"A dog teaches a boy fidelity, perseverance, and to turn around three times before lying down."

Robert Benchley

**Chris-Mas Pup**

Anyone familiar with boarding kennels knows that Christmas is a busy time, to put it mildly. We housed around two hundred dogs and fifty cats over the Christmas holidays, and turned away many hundreds more. Many made reservations a year in advance, after being put on a waiting list and learning their lesson.

Christmas was a little different in our business. We would open a package; check on the progress in the kennel, etc. This particular Christmas, my husband was in the kennel when our front doorbell rang. The kids and I looked at each other with dismay. Surely even the most inconsiderate of customers wouldn't interrupt our family on Christmas morning.

I opened the door to find a young man, in his mid-thirties with a child of about eight years old. She had tears streaming down her cheeks. Assuming these were people wanting to pick up their dog, I informed them that the kennel was closed for the holiday. He then told me he had a dog he needed to get rid of. I said we were in the boarding business, but I was certain the Humane Society could help him after the holiday. With this, he informed me he had no intention of going any further, and that he would just "let the puppy go in the street" if we didn't take him. Since the kennel is located on a six-lane insanely busy road, that was a death sentence.

I turned to see my daughter, with an imploring expression, handing me a slip lead. I followed the "gentleman" to his truck, and in the back was a shepherd mix puppy about eight months of age. The dog looked as terrified as the girl looked upset. I immediately placed the slip lead around his neck, and he gratefully came with me. I had all I could do to refrain from saying "This child will probably become a burden at some point too. Would you like me to take her off your hands as well?" And I probably would have, but for the fear that he would take the dog and let him loose to be run over, or worse, take his wrath out on the child. I simply watched as they drove away.

Shaken, I returned to the living room, new dog in tow. Our own animals, quite used to strangers, simply looked at me like…"what, another one?" My husband then came in from the kennel, took one look, and said "I'm afraid to ask". Of course, we had not a pen in the kennel…or room at the Inn. Our manager was kind enough to take "Chris" home until we could find room after some of our guests went home. Her dogs, like ours, were used to newcomers.

Chris' Christmas was a much happier one than he would have had, I'm sure. He was a delightful pup; leery of men, understandably, but affectionate once he learned he was safe with us. Everyone in the kennel took pity on him, and he got his share of bones, treats, and love. Once things settled down, we took Chris to The Open Door Animal Sanctuary, a no-kill shelter that we knew to be a caring, well run facility for homeless pets. Of course, they had no room, either, but after hearing Chris' story, they took pity on him, and us. We followed up, and learned that Chris finally got a good home, which he so richly deserved.

Since it often appears how people treat animals is a reflection on how they treat children, I often wonder how that poor child made out in life. I pray the most traumatic thing that happened to her was watching her puppy given away to a stranger, after threatening to kill it. I somehow doubt that this is the case. I only hope there was an Open Door Sanctuary out there for her, a safe haven from the cruelties of her world.

Sometimes holidays bring out the worst or best in people. The cruelty and selfishness of one only brings out the devotion and caring of others. My eternal thanks to the wonderful folks who volunteer at The Open Door Sanctuary, and all of the other people who step up to make this world a better place for pets and people.

*"Every boy should have two things: a dog and a mother willing to let him have one."*

Anonymous

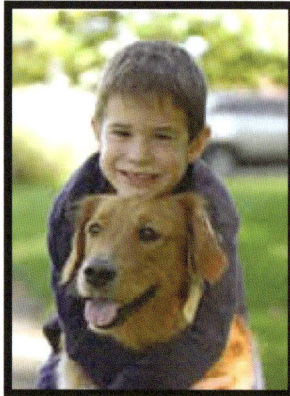

*"Every boy who has a dog should also have a mother, so the dog can be fed regularly."*

Anonymous

**Sleeping With Your Dog**

Now I lay me down to sleep,
The king-size bed is soft and deep.
I sleep right in the center groove
My human being can hardly move!

I've trapped her legs, she's tucked in tight
And here is where I pass the night.
No one disturbs me or dares intrude
'Till morning comes and "I want food!"

I sneak up slowly to begin
My nibbles on my human's chin.
She wakes up quickly,
I have sharp teeth-

I'm a puppy, don't you see?
For the morning's here
And it's time to play
I always seem to get my way.

So thank you Lord for giving me
This human person that I see,
The one who hugs and holds me tight
And shares her bed with me at night!

**Unknown**

Havana

"He is your friend, your partner, your defender, your dog. You are his life, his love, his leader. He will be yours, faithful and true, to the last beat of his heart. You owe it to him to be worthy of such devotion."

*Unknown*

**Hans & Gretel**

Often people relocating to the St. Louis area need a kennel before anything else. Many times newcomers are building a house or looking for an apartment, and it is much easier to accomplish this while the dog is safe and sound in a boarding facility.

A delightful couple moving to our area from Holland was such an example. They had temporary housing at the Residence Inn while house hunting, and left their beautiful Bouviers with us.

Hans and Gretel had been boarded in Holland prior to their departure, and we were instructed that they be boarded side by side, as they were previously, because neither were neutered or spayed and Gretel had just come into season before arriving to the states.

One morning while I was getting ready to open the office, my husband Ed called me to come down. When I walked into the grooming room, there stood three of the girls, each one holding a puppy. Beside them was a proud Gretel, smugly licking her new off-spring. They were obviously purebred Bouviers, however when we showed them to Hans, he seemed unimpressed. Apparently the kennel in Holland chose to put them together, rather than following the owner's instructions.

Once the shock wore off and the pups were checked and pronounced healthy, it was my job to inform the owners. I placed the call, and told the wife that I was calling from Williamsburg. Her immediate question was "Are my Bouviers Okay?" To which I replied "Oh, yes Mam...all FIVE of them are doing very well."

After a long, pardon the pun, pregnant pause, the owner wanted to come visit her new family. When it was obvious to them that these were, in fact, Hans and Gretel's kids, shock turned to delight with the realization of how much purebred Bouviers are worth! The pups more than covered the cost of the lengthy board bill, and everyone went home happy, even Hans and Gretel.

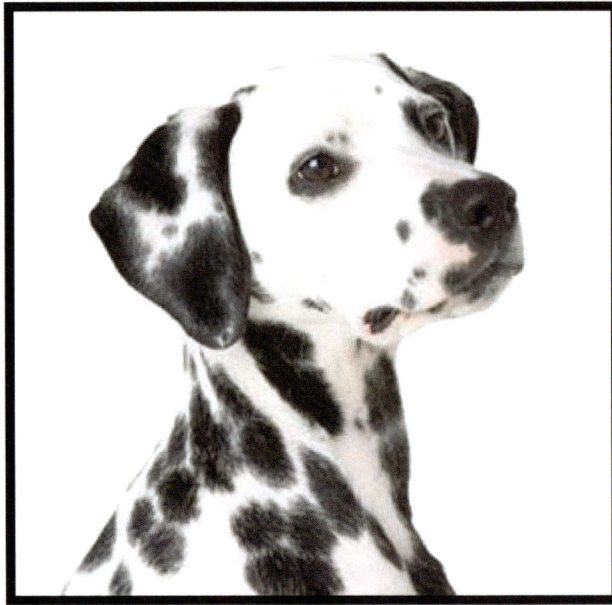

"If a dog will not come to you after having looked you in the face, you should go home and examine your conscience."

Woodrow Wilson

If you can start the day without caffeine,
If you can get going without pep pills,
If you can always be cheerful, ignoring aches and pains,
If you can resist complaining and boring people with your troubles,
If you can eat the same food every day and be grateful for it,
If you can understand when your loved ones are too busy to give you any time,
If you can take criticism and blame without resentment,
If you can ignore a friend's limited education and never correct him,
If you can resist treating a rich friend better than a poor friend,
If you can conquer tension without medical help,
If you can relax without liquor,
If you can sleep without the aid of drugs,
…Then You Are Probably The Family Dog!

**Mrs. Sykes & 1<sup>st</sup> Grade Class**
**Carman Trails Elementary School**

## Field Trips

Many times during the mid '80's through the late 90's the kennel had grade school classes and brownie troops schedule a visit. The children always seemed to enjoy the animals, and I welcomed the opportunity to give a little talk on the responsibilities of pet ownership. During these field trips, I usually baked cookies, in the shape of milk bones, for the kids. They got a kick out of eating their "bones", and the mess was minimal in the scheme of things.  We usually would give packets with items donated by pet companies, so they had something to take home besides memories.

I would frequently allow, with the owner's permission, certain pets to come out and play with the children.  Of course, one had to be careful they weren't too big to hurt the children, or too fragile to risk injury.  Usually I also added one of our pets in the mix, as they were used to strangers, and loved the extra attention and treats.

The women who guided these outings were to be commended for their patience.  Mrs. Sykes first grade class were frequent visitors, as were brownie troop #1843 from Carman Trails Elementary School.  Not once did they neglect to send thank you notes, which remain to this day near and dear to my heart, as do these wonderful kids and their mentors.

## Notes From The Little People

"Thank you for letting us look at the dog's and cat's we had fun. Thak you for letting us have dog boen cookie's and book's I liked Lucy."

"Thank you for the dog bone cookes and I liket that dofermen and the white dog named TJ and the best is that pootdle I sew I liket is that Chinese dog."

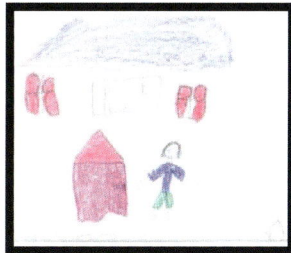

"Thank you for the cooke I liked them! And I liked Likrush and Lise. I got to go now."

"Thank you for the cuces and I likeed whene Likrish eat out of my hand ann it felt funnee. But I likeed whene the big dog brked at me. And I sowe a dog that looked like mike's dog his name was Radre."

"I liked the dog that was geted blow dryered.  He was nise.  And I liked the blak lab.  The End"

"My fafite prt at the cenolse is wen we saw the dogs out side."

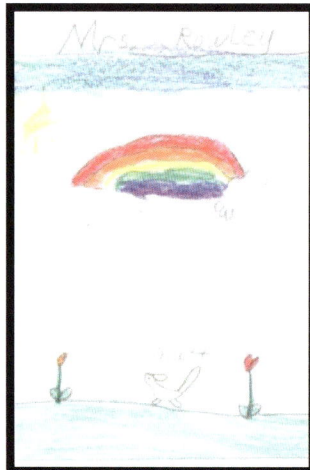

"I liked when we got to see Molly she wus ckuoot.  Thin we got to see a lot uve dogs."

"At the kennels the dog taked to me.  I was lafing!"

## Loyalty

You can't buy loyalty, they say,
I bought it, though, the other day.

You can't buy friendships, tried and true
Well, just the same, I bought that, too.

I made my bid, and on the spot
Bought love and faith, and a whole job lot

Of happiness, so all in all
The purchase price was pretty small.

I bought a single trusting heart
That gave devotion from the start.

If you think these things are

NOT FOR SALE

Buy a brown-eyed puppy with a wagging tail.

Unknown

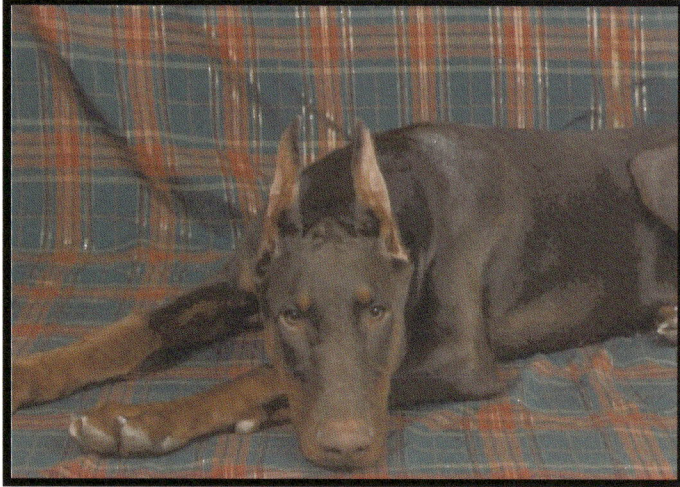

Hunter

While it seems that I'm including a lot of Doberman's in these stories, there is good reason. There have been more Doberman's in my life than any other breed, so I suppose it's only natural to have a soft spot in my heart for them. Besides, they have such a bad rap for being overly aggressive, I think it's good for people to get to know their silly side.

Our kennel manager, after becoming familiar with every existing breed, also fell in love with Dobes. It was normal for her to bring her dogs with her to work, as long as there were a couple of empty pens available.

Her huge red male by the name of Hunter weighed in at well over 100 pounds. He wasn't the least bit over weight, just tall, big boned, muscular, and a massive but beautiful specimen of the breed. He had one little thing that turned him into a quivering mass of apprehension: The Bath!

Being a good canine Mom, Aimee bathed her pets often. When at work, she had at her disposal an elevated bathtub, with a shampoo machine and blower for drying so it was the obvious choice to do this chore at the kennel. On her lunch hour, she often gave the pets a bath. But when it was Hunter's turn, she would let him out of the pen and say, "Bath time."

The "Magic Word" having been uttered, Hunter would seem to shrink to Miniature Pincher size, attempt to look invisible, and literally slither across the grooming room floor in search of an exit. More often than not, this was just one of their games. Then Aimee would announce "Kidding!" at which point Hunter would pull himself up to his full height, and jump for joy, dashing exuberantly around the grooming room in celebration of his pardon.

Hunter suffered through many real baths in between, but whenever the staff needed a good laugh, we could always count on Hunter the Clown, and his Fake Bath Time.

*"I hope if dogs ever take over the world, and they chose a king, they don't just go by size, because I bet there are some Chihuahuas with some good ideas."*

*Jack Handy*

*Deep Thoughts*

**Inscription of the Monument of a Newfoundland Dog**

**Near this spot are deposited the remains of one who**
**possessed Beauty without Vanity,**
**Strength without Insolence,**
**Courage without Ferocity,**
**and all the Virtues of Man,**
**without his Vices.**
**This Praise, which would be unmeaning**
**Flattery if inscribed over human**
**ashes is but a just tribute to the Memory**
**of Boatswain, a Dog.**

**Lord Byron**

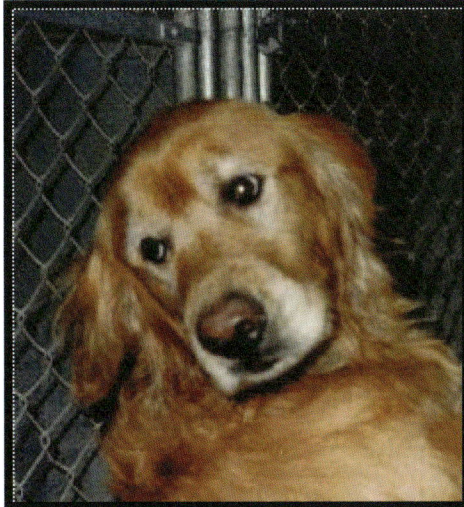

**Magnum**

Another special Golden Retriever who won our hearts was Magnum. He was a frequent border, but what set him apart from most was his mode of transportation. He usually arrived in a chauffeured limo.

Rarely were we given any notice of his arrival. Usually his owner would call as he was en route. Which was fine with us. His shots were always up to date, and he required little more than the average TLC. It was a little discombobbeling to a new office worker who would answer the phone, acquire a puzzled look, and hang up. Before they could question it, we would guess: Magnum's on his way? And, of course, he was.

Magnum always, bar none, received the full treatment before going home: bath, brush, nail trim, etc. When he left with the chauffeur, he always looked like a million dollars.

More often than not, within a couple of hours, we would receive another call saying that Magnum was on his way back to the kennel. After a time, we learned that it wasn't that his owner was unhappy with our grooming, it was simply that Magnum had gone home and rolled in the mud shortly after arrival. Hence, his second bath of the day.

Secretly, we just thought he missed his friends at Williamsburg and wanted to come back for more companionship and TLC!

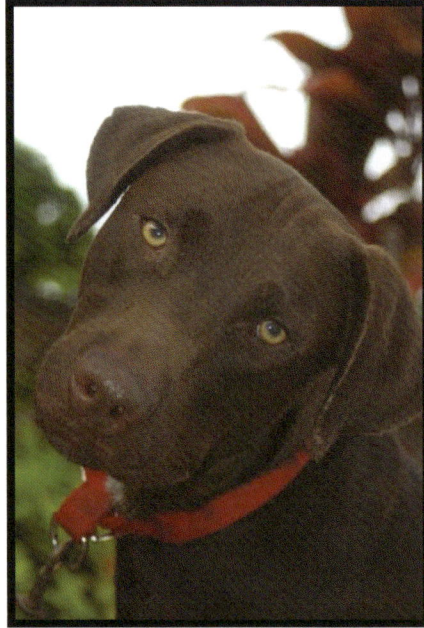

*"No matter how little money and how few possessions you own, having a dog makes you rich."*

*Louis Sabin*

*"What counts is not necessarily the size of the dog in the fight; it's the size of the fight in the dog."*

Dwight D. Eisenhower

## Walkin' In a Doggie Wonderland

Dog tags ring, are you listenin'?
In the lane, snow is glistenin',
It's yellow, NOT white, I've been there tonight,
Marking up my Winter Wonderland.

Smell that tree?  That's my fragrance,
It's a sign for wandering vagrants;
"Avoid where I pee, it's MY pro-per-ty!
Marked up as my Winter Wonderland."

In the meadow Dad will build a snowman,
Following the classical design;
Then I'll lift my leg and let it go, Man,
So all the world will know that it's Mine!

Straight from me to the fence post,
Flows my natural incense boast;
"Stay off my TURF, this small piece of earth,
I marked it as my Winter Wonderland."

Unknown

**Moon Shadow & Casey**

The Dr. and his wife had been good customers of our kennel for many years when they adopted yet another pet, a kitten named Moon Shadow. Black as the ace of spades, Moon Shadow had enormous yellow eyes. He was an extremely playful kitten, and loved to get into everything and anything available to him. Unfortunately, he was adopted shortly before the Christmas holidays.

This couple loved to entertain during the holidays. Their lovely and spacious home was the perfect place to elaborately decorate, with high ceilings, mahogany mantels, and a host of beautiful glass cabinets and curios. As was the tradition each Christmas season, a huge tree was placed in each room where entertaining was to take place: living room, den, library, dining room, and foyer.

Much to the dismay of the family, Moon Shadow proceeded to destroy each, one by one. Precious glass ornaments hit the floor like miniature bombs, exploding pieces of brilliantly colored glass throughout the room as he shimmied up the tree out of reach of a livid owner.

Thus began Moon Shadow's annual trip to Williamsburg. On the first of December, he would arrive to spend the holidays with us each and every year of his long life, to be picked up sometime after the first of the year, when all of the trees had been taken down, and the ornaments packed away for another year. We always looked forward to Moon's exile, as it were, and loved having him be a part of our holiday season at the kennel.

The Dr. and his wife also had teenagers at the time, and a great Airedale named Casey. One day when he arrived home, he tripped over Casey lying in the hallway. It must have been a frustrating day at the office, because he turned to his wife and exclaimed "I don't understand why we have to have all of these animals. They cost a lot of money, they don't contribute anything to the family, and all they do is lie around taking up space." To which she smiled and answered, "Have you looked at our children lately?" It was the last time the doctor ever complained about the pets!

"If you are a dog and your owner suggests
that you wear a sweater...suggest that he wear a tail."


Fran Lebowitz

Hilde

*"The dog is a yes-animal. Very popular with people who can't afford a yes man."*

*Robertson Davies*
*Canadian author*

"Dogs laugh, but they laugh with their tails. What puts man in a higher state of evolution is that he has got his laugh on the right end."

Max Eastman

**Niffel**

We had some of the cutest mixed breeds on the planet stay at our kennel.

The difference was, in those days, a mix breed was simply that. It was not a Lhasadoodle, a Maltzu, a Labrapoo, or any of the designer breeds which people pay an arm and a leg for today. After all, a rose by any other name is still a mixed breed. And is that something to be ashamed of? I happen to think that some of our originals were the greatest. And like true designer dogs, they really were one of a kind. We even had one named Gucci for that reason. It used to be that people took pride in their original dogs. Now it seems we try to clone them into breeds never accepted by the AKC. Any Humane Society or ASPCA in America has an abundance of these adorable, personable mutts up for adoption at way less than designer dog prices. This way, we encourage saving the homeless critters, rather than encouraging profits from producing even more mixed breeds than we can adequately provide for.

One of our most precious "originals" was a little poodle/something mix named Niffel. His owner was an NFL linesman…hence the name. Niffel was multi-colored, and usually came to us clipped about three inches long all over. He was just an adorable little rag-a-muffin, and we all were so fond of him.

One day he came into the kennel, well, humiliated. He had been to a new groomer who just didn't understand Niffel's personality. They gave him what only can be described as an unfortunate hair cut. When the kennel help would pass his pen, they would automatically look at the gate card, since they didn't recognize the dog. The reaction was, "Niffel! What happened to you?" Niffel would put his paws over his head, and look just like anyone suffering from total embarrassment.

As his coat began to grow back, our old Niffel's charming character returned. It just goes to show how devastating a truly bad hair day, or month, can be!

**From the Diaries of Dogs & Cats**

**Excerpts from a Dog's Diary:**

8:00   AM  - Dog food!  My favorite thing!
9:30   AM  - A car ride!  My favorite thing!
9:40   AM  - A walk in the park!  My favorite thing!
10:30 AM - Got rubbed and petted!  My favorite thing!
12:00 PM - Lunch!  My favorite thing!
1:00   PM - Played in the yard!  My favorite thing!
3:00   PM - Wagged my tail!  My favorite thing!
5:00   PM - Milk Bones!  My favorite thing!
7:00   PM - Got to play ball!  My favorite thing!
8:00   PM - Wow! Watched TV with the people!  My favorite thing!
11:00 PM - Sleeping on the bed!  My favorite thing!

**Excerpts from a Cat's Diary:**

My captors continue to taunt me with bizarre little dangling objects.

They dine lavishly on fresh meat, while the other inmates and I are fed hash or some sort of dry nuggets.  Although I make my contempt for the rations perfectly clear, I nevertheless must eat something in order to keep up my strength.  The only thing that keeps me going is my dream of escape.  In an attempt to disgust them, I once again vomit on the carpet.

Today I decapitated a mouse and dropped its headless body at their feet.

I had hoped this would strike fear into their hearts, since it clearly demonstrates what I am capable of. However, they merely made condescending comments about what a "good little hunter" I am.

There was some sort of assembly of their accomplices tonight. I was placed in solitary confinement for the duration of the event. However, I could hear the noises and smell the food. I overheard that my confinement was due to the power of "allergies." I must learn what this means, and how to use it to my advantage.

Today I was almost successful in an attempt to assassinate one of my tormentors by weaving around his feet as he was walking. I must try this again tomorrow – but at the top of the stairs.

I am convinced that the other prisoners here are flunkies and snitches. The dog receives special privileges. He is regularly released – and seems to be more than willing to return. He is obviously retarded.

The bird has got to be an informant. I observe him communicate with the guards regularly. I am certain that he reports my every move. My captors have arranged protective custody for him in an elevated cage, so he is safe.
For now…

Hamilton

Dog and cats weren't the only creatures boarded at Williamsburg. We had our share of the exotic, and of those Hamilton the Vietnamese Pot-Bellied Pig was the most memorable.

Hamilton, Ham for short, was boarded in the kennel proper, as he wasn't one of the pigs who were litter-trained. He wanted to go outside every three hours just like the rest of the kennel. One problem with that was that Hamilton was black, and very prone to sunburn. We monitored his exercises closely, as he could only be outside a few minutes, while the majority of the kennel were outside about 20 minutes each time.

Another problem with Ham was that his family always wanted him bathed prior to going home. At that time, the grooming room was just off of the office, where customers came to pick up and drop off their pets.

We were never certain whether Hamilton hated his baths or not, but one thing was for sure: he squealed at the top of his lungs from the time he was put into the tub to the time he was taken out. I'm not referring to a little soft squeal; I'm referring to a noise at about the same intensity as a siren!

This definitely was not good for business! Customers entering the office during Ham's bath time looked horrified, as if they had entered a slaughter house! We found ourselves constantly opening the door to the grooming room to assure them we were not, in fact, killing off our clients.

Finally, someone discovered the solution to the problem: feed him! The old proverb "eats like a pig" really is true. From that point on, we assigned two people to bath Ham: the Bather and the Feeder. We could stretch a handful of food to last an entire QUIET bath! Everyone was happy: customers that didn't hear the squealing; staff that didn't feel guilty; owners with a clean pig; and Hamilton with a full belly!

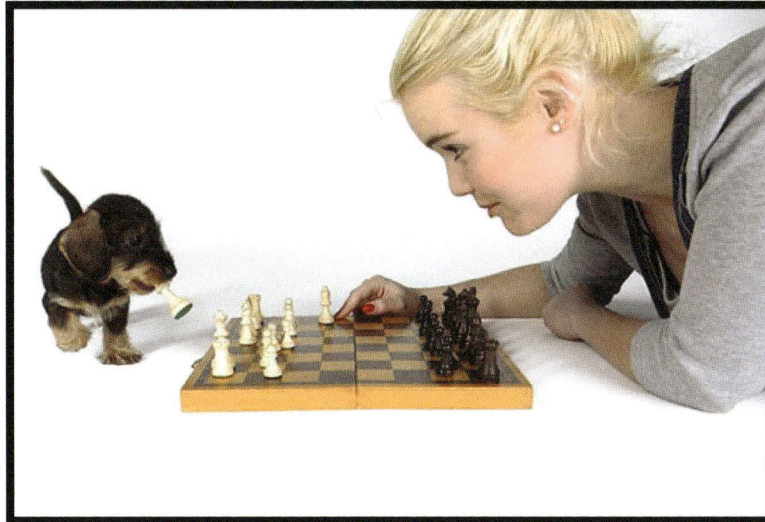

"My dog is usually pleased with what I do, because she is not infected with the concept of what I "should" be doing."

Lonzo Idolswine

Chico

At Williamsburg, as I'm sure in most kennels, we had some "code words". In other words, if you put "bites" on a dogs file, the owner would be upset, and defensive… "My dog doesn't bite!" But in order to keep from having a staff member get bit, we deemed it necessary.

Sometimes a dog would just be frightened upon entering the kennel, and then settle down and be fine once tucked in. Other times, the dog would, predictably, bite. You could almost tell by the look in a dog's eye, but not always.

We always checked each pet entering the kennel or cattery for any problems when coming in. This might include fleas and ticks, cuts or abrasions, ear infections, etc. It was essential to catch these troubles to resolve, or keep an eye on during their stay. Some dogs, however, were not thrilled about having someone other than their owners playing "touchy-feely" with their bodies.

Our code word for dogs and cats that might/could/will bite was "Slow!" When the staff was summoned to the office to get the pet, our secretary would caution that we "go slowly with Buffy". We would explain to the owner that Buffy was a little nervous coming in, so it was just a reminder to take our time with him.

Upon one such occasion, a little Chihuahua named Chico was coming in for a stay. Chico had an attitude. Not uncommon for Chihuahuas, he had a Napoleon Complex. The problem with small dogs is that they don't always give you much of a warning when they're feeling cantankerous. Such was the case with Chico.

My husband Ed came up to get Chico, since we were swamped with customers at the time. I was on the phone taking a reservation, and didn't pay that much attention to the circumstances. In the height of chaos, Nancy simply overlooked the large, red "SLOW!" on Chico's file.

We had Dutch doors that opened from the office to the grooming room, and when the dog was finished with the check-in, we would open the top door so the family could say goodbye. When Nancy (the receptionist) realized her neglect, she hurriedly opened the door to warn Ed. As she opened it, she said, "Oh Ed, by the way, we go slowly with Chico." With this, we all looked in the grooming room, where Chico was dangling a foot off the table, teeth firmly clamped onto Ed's index finger. Ed calmly looked up and said, "Thanks, Nancy". We were all grateful that Chico wasn't a Rottweiler!

"I care not for a man's religion whose dog and cat are not the better for it."

Abraham Lincoln

**Buffy**

Some dogs just have an attitude.  Buffy was a feisty little package; some Pomeranian, and I suspect, some Chihuahua.  I think he found out early in life that his owners were accommodating people, willing to sacrifice all for his total happiness.   Once engrained in the role of authority in the household, he merely allowed them to share the same roof…if they were obedient, that is.

It was a common occurrence to have the owner bring Buffy in, her legs covered with butterfly bandages from the many teeth marks.  Each time she would get out of line, Buffy would make sure she paid dearly.  As much as she loved him, deep down there was fear as well, and certainly with good reason.  Once her husband had the pure audacity to sit in Buffy's favorite chair and was bit so viciously he was put in the hospital for several days.  Who says big bites don't come in small packages?

Usually the wife was the brave one to retrieve Buffy from the kennel.  Often the office was filled with clients, both coming and going, who would be very confused at the reaction when the kennel attendants brought Buffy out.  While waiting, the owner would always ask, "Is he in a good mood?"  Then, when we handed her the leash, she rarely reached down to pet him without getting a welcome back bite.

Our kennel manager, Aimee, was the best of caring people, but also knew how to reason with the contrary critters.  Early in his boarding career, Aimee put Buffy in his place.  She simply took his head in her hands (so he couldn't snap), looked him straight in the eye, and said, "Don't, in your wildest dreams, even think about biting me!"  As I watched, Buffy's eyes took on a reflection of understanding.  First was shock, that someone would actually suggest they were in charge.  Next came resignation.  From that moment on, Buffy never gave any of us a moment's aggravation.

I only hope that after Buffy went to doggy heaven (or hell) that their next choice of pet turned out to be less of a challenge for them.  Or that they read some books on how to become more assertive in the human/pet relationship area.   No one should ever have to put up with a "Buffy" in their life!

**Paws to Ponder…**

**Original Pet Names:**

Eiffel Towerman
Bum Wrap
DC (Damn Cat)
Teton (Great Pyrenees)
Gucci (an original)

Baseball players' pets:
Slider (Keith Hernandez)
Lou Brock (Tito Landrum)
Sluggo (Jack Clark)

**Named after where they were found:**

Schnuck's (local grocery)
Freeway
U Haul

**And when:**

Friday
Christmas
Wednesday

**And what saved their lives:**

Gator (Gatorade)

**And Pairs:**

Laverne & Shirley
Bill & Hillary
Brandy & Soda

**Original Foods Brought In:**

An apple a day (to keep the vet away)
Domino's Pizza
Breaded chicken breasts
Canned string beans
Prime rib
Grapes
Carrots
Prime rib
Fish filets
Kentucky Fried Chicken
Big Mac

**Recycled Items:**
(some requiring vet assistance)

Underwear
Golf ball
Pantyhose

**Things Brought In With Pets:**

Negligee'
Photos of family
Baseball glove
Jeans
Underwear
Limoge china

# OJ

While some people seem to believe that leaving a dog in a kennel for an extended period is cruel, many dogs actually love the chaos and social aspect of seeing many new friends. Dog are, after all, pack animals, and whether their pack has two legs are four sometimes they enjoy a change of scene.

One of our favorite long-term boarders was a big black lab named OJ. Unlike his namesake, our OJ was sweet, gentle, unassuming, and above all, loved to visit the kennel. He would get excited when his owner would pull into the parking lot, and if the front window was down on the car, he would jump right out and wait at the office door for his owner to catch up.

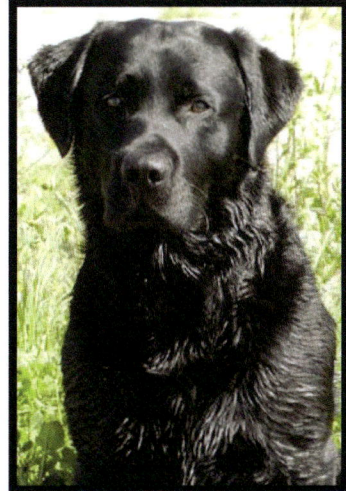

The usual check-in policy was that the office staff rang for a kennel attendant to come pick up or to retrieve a pet. However, when OJ arrived, he would bang with his front paw on the door to the grooming room. When the attendant opened it, he would sprint past, heading straight for the kennel in a mad dash. I think in his mind, he wanted to choose which pen was his on any given stay. Of course, with The Juice, as he was affectionately called, this was allowed.

The Juice's usual stay ranged from three to six months. His family explained that they never felt guilty about leaving him, as it was obvious he was more than enthusiastic about coming, yet always happy to see them when they returned.

After about the first month or so, he would invent games to break the daily routine. One such game was to choose his own exercise schedule. Every three hours throughout the day, we would open the guillotine doors one by one for the dogs to go into their own outside pens for some fresh air and exercise. Once so inclined, OJ would just wag his tail when his turn came to go out but refuse to budge. About twenty minutes later, when everyone was coming in, there he would be standing by his door waiting to go out.

One Sunday when the kennel was closed to the public, but everyone was still working in the back we heard a knock on the front door. It was an employee from one of the neighboring businesses, who was concerned that all of the other dogs were inside except for one black lab. He said he thought we must have forgotten him, but we assured him that was not the case. "That's just OJ", we explained. "He walks to the beat of a different drum."

"*You think dogs will not be in heaven? I tell you, they will be there long before any of us.*"

*Robert Louis Stevenson*

**Phred**

My sister Kathi managed the kennel for years, so I feel her dog Phred deserves some space. He was truly a unique little guy, and a blessing to all who knew him.

Prior to coming home to manage the kennel when our parents retired, Kathi had an apartment in downtown St. Louis. One day when she was leaving her apartment, she noticed a little dog running lose in the street. He appeared to be a Dandy Dinmont mix; short and stocky with shaggy gray hair. Being from a pet-oriented family, she immediately set out to snare the little guy and return him safely home. He was wearing a collar, so she brought him the half mile or so to his home and rang the bell. The fellow who answered the door didn't seem at all grateful, and simply said, "Oh, he does that all the time."

Two weeks later, she came out again to find him in the gutter, apparently hit by a car, with an obviously broken leg. At this point, Kathi decided the owner's didn't deserve him, and tossed his collar into the trash. She took him to a vet, paid the bill, and Phred was her constant companion until the day he died.

Not only did Phred (P-Fred as we called him in the kennel) not wander, he never in his life needed a lead. He remained glued to Kathi's ankle at all times.

Phred would stay with us when Kathi was out of town, and we all so enjoyed his personality. When we would take a toy away from him, or simply play up that he was in the kennel, we would say, "What did they do to the baby?" and he would put on the biggest display of whining imaginable. Such a pathetic sight he would become!

Canines are more intelligent than anyone could ever imagine. It seems P-Fred knew there was a better life out there, and wouldn't rest until he found it. Unlike most humans, he did recognize goodness when it came, and was appreciative until the end of his days.

**Cayman**

*"A really companionable and indispensable dog is an accident of nature. You can't get it by breeding for it, and you can't buy it with money. It just happens along."*

*E. B. White*

*The Care and Training of a Dog*

"Heaven goes by favour.  If it went by merit, you would stay out and your dog would go in."

Mark Twain

Tigger & the Dogs

Our house cat, Tigger, came by us in all the wrong ways. Our manager, Aimee, came in one day with a basket of kittens her cat had delivered. They were varied in color, but one little guy was a soft muted yellow/beige with subtle stripes. He was the hellion of the lot: the first one out of the whelping box, always in to something or another.

When I said," I want that one," my husband Ed thought I'd lost my mind. I was always preaching that research was the best approach to pet ownership, and to never, never get a pet spur of the moment. It was a commitment of roughly 15 years, and should never be taken lightly.

When he asked me why we needed a cat, I said that our feline owner clients must think we're prejudiced to canines, and besides, we already owned numerous litter boxes and had kitten chow.

We had two miniature Poodles at the time, one of which was blind. When introduced, they both seemed to accept the kitten alright, but Tigger soon learned which dog he could aggravate. The "ditsy" young one, Licorice, was fair game, but stay out of Pepper's way. After all, being blind gives you the instant right of way in any given circumstance.

Tigger was a smart though feisty kitten. He just loved to hide behind the banister and pounce out when he saw someone coming down the stairs. Though declawed, he got a real charge out of scaring the humans. He also loved to get onto a chair and pounce on Licorice, the younger dog.

One day I observed Tigger in his attack position on the chair, paused and ready to pounce. The only problem was that the target he was taking aim for was Pepper, not Licorice. In mid-air, he also realized his faux pas. He literally wilted in mid-air and sort of floated to the floor. In typical cat fashion, he meandered away, as if he hoped no one noticed his error.

It was great fun observing the interaction of this trio. I have always wondered if people who never owned a pet had any conception of the education they have missed by not allowing these wonderful creatures into their lives.

Tazzie          Peggy Sue          Frankie          Lucy

## The Frenchies

When a breeder would board their dogs, which wasn't often due to the cost and chaos, it was quite an ordeal.  One of our favorites was a wonderful lady who bred French Bulldogs.

If you've never seen a Frenchie, they are little dogs, and come in a variety of colors. They have short snouts, and make a sort of snorting sound, much like little piglets. They have wonderful dispositions and an abundance of personality.

When this particular family would come in, all involved wanted to be certain that we got the correct gate card with the proper dog.  The gate card goes on the kennel door, and has the dog's name, feeding and medical instructions on it.  Since some of the dogs were on medication and some weren't, this was of utmost importance.  Despite the fact that some looked so similar, they all had their own personalities.  Still, the check-in process could be quite confusing.

The owner would bring in one at a time, and announce, "Here's Frankie".  Then, "Here's Tazzie", etc.  Once everyone was settled in, we would take her back into the kennel, with them all lined up in a row, to make sure we had everyone duly labeled.  Then we would begin the process of taking food and medical instructions.

Any other clients that happened to come into the office during this process would be amazed, and grateful that their check-in, relatively speaking, seemed so simple.

Going home was even more fun, with an office full of little "piggies" running around happily snorting hello's to their owners.  What fun little dogs these were, and how we enjoyed them bringing so much pleasure into our lives.

"I once decided not to date a guy because he wasn't excited to meet my dog. I mean, this was like not wanting to meet my mother."

Bonnie Schacter
Founder of the Single Pet Owner's Society Singles Group

**Red Baron**

At one point in our operation of the kennel, we had a wonderful secretary named Nancy. Like all of our employees, Nancy and her husband Jim were dog lovers, as well as owners. One of her most memorable pets was a Pointer named Baron.

Baron was without a doubt one of the best "doggie actors" we've known. If there were an Academy Award for the canine set, it would have been displayed on Nancy's mantel.

One example was the waterbed, which Baron was not allowed on in case he became rambunctious and would spring a leak in the plastic cover. Daily upon arriving home from work, Nancy would find Baron curled up in his L.L. Beanbag on the floor, looking for all the world like the picture of innocence. The dead give-away, of course, was that the waterbed was still frantically sloshing from side to side. Baron would look at it, then look around the room as if in search of the culprit that could have possibly made that happen.

One day while Jim was hosing the driveway, he happened to turn and accidentally squirt Baron straight in the face with the nozzle turned up full blast. While Nancy and Jim watched in horror, Baron keeled over on his side, and lay there, stiff as a board. Frantic, they ran to him, and tried to revive him to no avail. They wrapped him in a blanket and carried him to their bed. Sure this was some sort of a heart attack, they called their veterinarian for an emergency appointment.

After a thorough examination, the vet chuckled and gave them the good news. "There is absolutely nothing wrong with this dog," he said. "I'm sure at first he was stunned, but now he's decided that the attention was well worth the shock."

And sure enough, from that day forward, anytime Baron was reprimanded, or just didn't get his dinner on time, he would immediately crash to the floor, tongue lolling, and stiffen up as if rigor mortis had set in.

Members of The Academy: Take note!

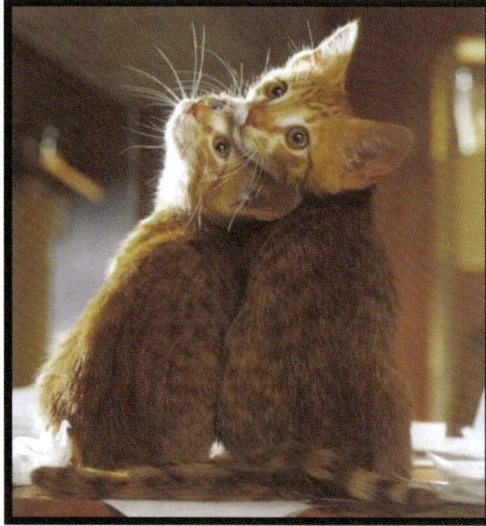

"A cat sees us as the dogs...
A cat sees himself as the human."

Unknown

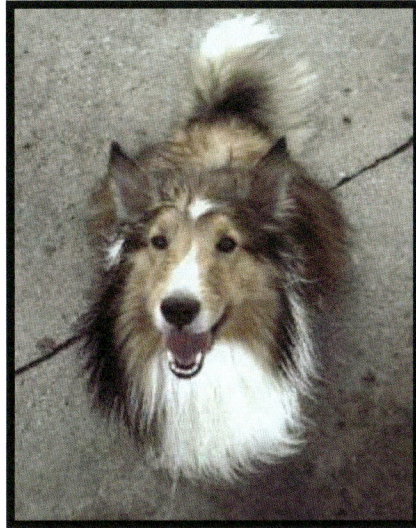

**Sadie**

The Dog Days of Summer is certainly an apt phrase for August in the boarding kennel business, at least in the Midwest. The season begins with Memorial Day. At this point, after a lull in January and February, it is exciting to begin to see huge lines to get in, as well as waiting lists. But by August, you're really ready for everyone to stay home!

We were a good-size kennel, accommodating at that time about 200 dogs and 30 cats. We never required a deposit as most of our customers were honest and only cancelled at the last minute if something sincerely came up to change their trip plans. Because of this, I was more than a little annoyed when a lady came in with one Sheltie, when she had made a reservation for two. When asked what happened to the second dog, she apologized and shared one of the most touching stories I'd ever been privileged to hear.

It seems our customer Mary was a realtor, and many times worked with families moving to the area. Sometimes they met Mary at her home when they would arrive in town after office hours. Over the past week, Mary had met with a couple that were relocating, and had an urgent need to find a house quickly. It was obvious to Mary that their young daughter, Beth, was severely autistic. Beth sat on the sofa, never moving or becoming antsy with the proceedings like a normal four-year-old might.

Mary and her husband were breeders of Shetland Sheep dogs, and still had one pup left from a recent litter, born about seven months prior. While the mother dog lay quietly on the floor, the pup, Sadie, was immediately drawn to little Beth. Sadie jumped up on the sofa along side of Beth, and waited until Beth seemed comfortable with this new agenda.

Beth's parents and Mary tried to work on housing, but were constantly distracted by what Sadie was attempting to accomplish. Within two hours, all were in tears as they watched Beth, who had never given direct eye contact to anyone, get down on the floor and begin to fondle and play with Sadie.

When the miraculous evening was finally coming to an end, they all walked out to the family car together. When little Beth was placed in her car seat in the back, amazingly, in jumped Sadie. The look she gave her owner was simple and easy to understand, even for people. It said, "Please...this is what I'm supposed to do."

I asked Mary what happened then, and she said, "What was I supposed to do? I said *Take good care of my puppy.*"

How could one be upset over the cancellation? Reservations are insignificant in the scheme of things. Changing the life of a child is monumental.

**Sarge**

An endearing quirk that some dogs possess is the ability to smile. They pull their lips back, and look for the world like a human grinning. While some breeds seem to have this tendency more than others, we've seen some great smilers in breeds large, medium, and small. Some produce an almost smirkish appearance, while others just plain grin from ear to ear.

Of all the smilers we've had through the years at Williamsburg, Sarge was without a doubt the all time winner. Just being an 85 pound Doberman was enough to get everyone's attention when he smiled, but his grin went beyond that. Sarge showed every tooth (fang!) in his massive head at the slightest hint of attention. All one had to do was say "Hi, Sarge" and he would literally beam.

Another talent of Sarge's was sitting up, a rare thing for a Doberman. He could balance himself, with his back totally straight like a poodle, and grin with pride at his accomplishment.

Everyone at the kennel loved Sarge, and gave him every opportunity to have something to smile about. This only became a problem when we would show the kennel, and Sarge would terrify the visitor by flashing them one of his classic snarl-like faces.

The other time of concern happened when a new kennel attendant started work for us. We would send him back to bring Sarge up when the owner came for him, or for a bath, totally forgetting he was new. Before we knew it, a white-faced kid would come back shaking, and say "No way am I going in with THAT dog!"

## Where Did Pets Come From?

And Adam said, "Lord, when I was in the garden, you walked with me every day. Now I do not see you anymore. I am lonesome here and it is difficult for me to remember how much you love me."

And God said, "No problem! I will create a companion for you that will be with you forever and who will be a reflection of my love for you, so that you will know I love you, even when you cannot see me. Regardless of how selfish and childish and unlovable you may be, this new companion will accept you as you are and will love you as I do, in spite of yourself."

And God created a new animal to be a companion for Adam. And it was a good animal. And God was pleased.

And the new animal was pleased to be with Adam and he wagged his tail. And Adam said, "But Lord, I have already named all the animals in the Kingdom and all the good names are taken and I cannot think of a name for this new animal."

And God said, "No problem! Because I have created this new animal to be a reflection of my love for you, his name will be a reflection of my own name, and you will call him DOG."

And Dog lived with Adam and was a companion to him and loved him. And Adam was comforted. And God was pleased. And Dog was content and wagged his tail.

After a while, it came to pass that Adam's guardian angel came to the Lord and said, "Lord, Adam has become filled with pride. He struts and preens like a peacock and he believes he is worthy of adoration. Dog has indeed taught him that he is loved, but no one has taught him humility."

And the Lord said, "No problem! I will create for him a companion who will be with him forever and who will see him as he is. The companion will remind him of his limitations, so he will know that he is not worthy of adoration."

And God created CAT to be a companion to Adam. And Cat would not obey Adam.

And when Adam gazed into Cat's eyes, he was reminded that he was not the supreme being. And Adam learned humility.

And God was pleased. And Adam was greatly improved.

And CAT did not care one way or the other.

Author Unknown

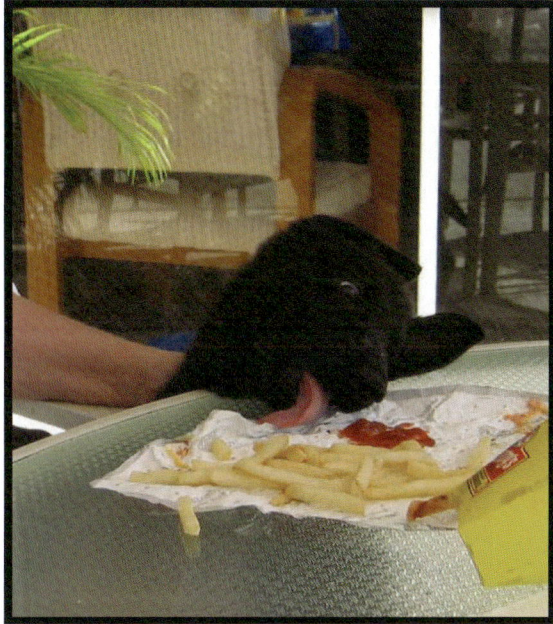

*"Never trust a dog to watch your food."*

*Unknown*

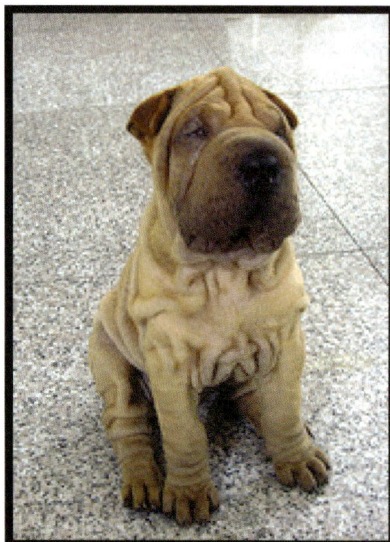

**Sluggo**

Among the many sports celebrities who have boarded with us throughout the years was a Cardinal first baseman named Jack Clark who was the definite star of the team for years in St. Louis. When he first came to our kennel, he and his beautiful wife had recently acquired an adorable Shar Pei pup, appropriately named Sluggo.

The Clark's were impressed with the kennel, but had some concerns about Sluggo keeping up with his obedience training, since he would be with us for the entire Spring Training of the team, which at that time was held in St. Petersburg, Florida. A trainer was contacted who was willing to come to the kennel to work with him several times per week. She would have her husband use a video camera to record his lessons in the hope that it would be easier for the Clarks to keep up upon their return.

While Sluggo seemed to enjoy the training, he loved the kennel and seeing all of the other dogs. He always was so concerned he was missing something in the kennel, he had a short attention span during his lessons.

The kennel was exercised every three hours, and all of the dogs were allowed into their own outside pens to run back and forth and bark at each other. Whenever Sluggo would hear the other dogs romping and barking, he would try to end his lesson and join in the fun. The way he did this was to vigorously shake his head back and forth, causing all of his wrinkles to make a loud, flapping sound. As if that were his change of subject, he would abruptly head back to the exercise period he was missing.

We were all fans at Williamsburg, especially of the Cardinals, Jack Clark, and his endearing pup.

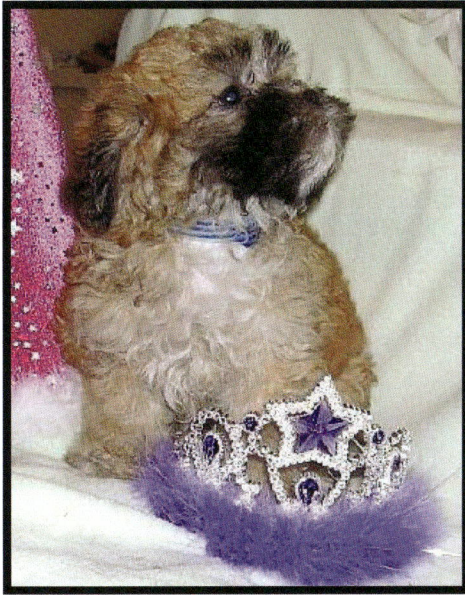

"My dog is half pit bull, half poodle.
Not much of a watchdog, but a vicious gossip!"

Craig Shoemaker

**Storm and the Sofa**

Before we bought the kennel, back in the '60's, the live-in Doberman of the time was Ch. Storm Von Vulcan. Storm was quite a character, and liked to test the limits of our endurance, and his ability to push the envelope.

One of the house rules that Storm had trouble accepting was the rule about only two-legged creatures belonged on the sofa. While all of our animals were allowed in our beds, we had replaced too many sofas and decided it was a necessary rule.

We would all be watching television in the evening, when Storm would nonchalantly back up to the sofa and park his rear end. When scolded, he would look at his feet, all four of which were on the ground. When we decided this was passable, he would then begin his "scootch" backward. Within a short time, he would have edged his back legs up, and only his front paws were touching the floor. We would correct him, and he would look at his front legs, then you, as if to say, "What's the problem? Can't you see my feet are on the floor?"

Of course, this would eventually lead to the lifting of his right paw. Now, only one toe of his left paw remained on the floor. We found that a dog will never take a correction seriously when you are rolling on the floor in gales of laughter!

"The great pleasure of a dog is that you may make a fool of yourself with him and not only will he not scold you, but he will make a fool of himself too."

Samuel Butler

### Tigger & the Window

House cats that have never been outside generally have no desire to wander.  After all, the only thing that they know of that exists "out there" are Veterinarians...and that doesn't inspire a desire to roam.

Our house cat, Tigger, was no exception.  Living on a nine lane road certainly precluded any thought of an outside cat, so after our dogs began to resemble pin cushions, Tigger was declawed, neutered and destined to spend life indoors.

Tigger seemed perfectly content with this.  He loved lying on the window sill and taunting the dogs who were coming into the kennel.  Suffice to say, he ruled the roost.  Even on the occasions when he was boarded, he acted as if he owned the cattery...which, in a manner of speaking, he did.

One day the kennel secretary called us into the office, saying a customer noticed a cat on the front porch of the house entrance.  Of course, we assured her it wasn't one of ours; we didn't "lose" cats.  Still, the secretary Sandy, a cat lover, decided to take a look.  She called me and said that the cat sure looked a lot like Tigger!

We had recently hired a painter in the house, and he had finished the windows, but neglected to latch the screen.  When Tigger took his spot on the sill and leaned all 16 pounds into the screen, it gave way and out he came onto the porch.  Thanks goodness it was on the first floor.  When I went out, there he was, smashed up against one of the columns with eyes the size of silver dollars.  I opened the front door, and he bolted in "like a bat out of Hell".

From that point on, not only did he never try to escape, when the door opened, he would run as far as he possibly could from the outside world.  No one could ever convince him the grass was greener on the other side of the door!

**Berkeley**

## Dog Proverbs

"To live long, eat like a cat, drink like a dog." (German Proverb)

"Beware of a silent dog and still water." (Latin Proverb)

"The greater love is a mother's, then comes a dog's, then a sweetheart's."(Polish Proverb)

"One dog barks at something, the rest bark at him." (Chinese Proverb)

"If you are a host to your guest, be a host to his dog also." (Russian Proverb)

"A house without either a cat or a dog is the house of a scoundrel." (Portuguese Proverb)

"Every dog is allowed one bite." (US Proverb)

If you stop every time a dog barks, your road will never end." (Saudi Arabian Proverb)

"Children aren't dogs; adults aren't gods." (Haitian Proverb)

"A good dog deserves a good bone." (US Proverb)

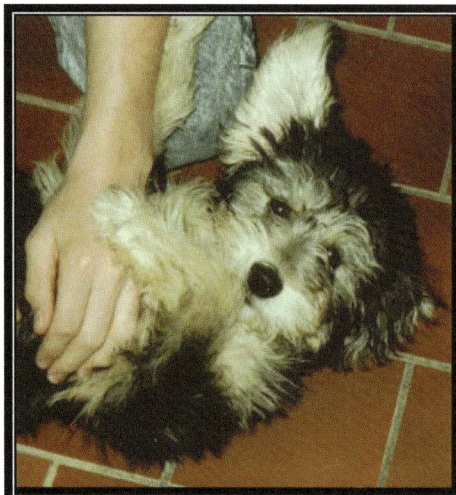

### Wee Willy

One busy summer day at the kennel, we received a call from our neighboring business, Kentucky Fried Chicken. The manager was calling to inform us that there was a dog under one of the cars in their parking lot and they thought it may be one of ours. After assuring them we didn't "lose" dogs, I decided to go take a look and see what the commotion was about.

I walked next door to the car in question and got down on my hands and knees to take a peek. Staring back at me with a panicked look was the cutest puppy I'd ever seen! I said' "Well, you're just a baby!" and out he bounded into my arms.

I carried him back to the kennel, after assuring the manager at KFC it really <u>wasn't</u> one of ours, but we'd take care of the situation. The staff fell immediately in love with the little guy, presumably part Airedale and part "whatever". He was dubbed Wee Willy, for Williamsburg.

After much spoiling by the staff, and us of course, we decided he had to have a really good home. We set out to find the perfect home for Wee Willy. We were successful, and Wee Willy continued to visit his surrogate parents at the kennel for many years. It was such a pleasure watching him grow. Wee Willy must be added to the list of big blessings in our lives.

"I like dogs better (than people). They give you unconditional love. They either lick your face or bite you, but you always know where they're coming from. With people, you never know which ones will bite. The difference between dogs and men is that you know where dogs sleep at night."
Greg Louganis

Waco & Peaches

One of our all time favorites was Waco, a tiny Yorkie with a wonderful disposition. Waco was a "mite" who weighed in at about 4 pounds. He did fairly well in the kennel, but didn't like it when all the dogs barked their greeting to new comers. This was prior to the addition of suites, and sometimes the kennel proper could be a noisy place.

Waco's family decided to add a kitten to the mix, and adopted Peaches, a beautiful feline the color of, you got it, peaches. Peaches and Waco became instant Buddies, always curled up with one another.

After some discussion with the family, it was decided that the cattery, where Peaches stayed, was a lot quieter than the kennel. Also, the two seemed very lonely without one another. We all made the decision to board them together, in the cattery, as the pens could be expanded so that Peaches still had privacy in the litter box.

The interesting part came during our many tours of the facility. People usually did a double-take when seeing an eight pound cat snuggled up with a four pound dog in a cat pen! They looked like the original Odd Couple, but the other cats just regarded Waco as a strange looking feline. They were the picture of contentment, and we loved them both.

"Dogs have given us their absolute all. We are the center of their universe. We are the focus of their love and faith and trust. They serve us in return for scraps. It is without a doubt the best deal man has ever made."


Roger Caras

A man and his dog were walking along a road. The man was enjoying the scenery, when it suddenly occurred to him that he was dead.

He remembered dying, and that the dog walking beside him had been dead for years. He wondered where the road was leading them.

After a while, they came to a high, white stone wall along one side of the road. It looked like fine marble. At the top of a long hill, it was broken by a tall arch that flowed in the sunlight.

When he was standing before it he saw a magnificent gate in the arch that looked like mother-of-pearl, and the street that led to the gate looked like pure gold. He and the dog walked toward the gate, and as he got closer, he saw a man at a desk to one side.

When he was close enough, he called out, "Excuse me, where are we?" "This is Heaven, sir," the man answered.

"Wow! Would you happen to have some water?" the man asked.

"Of course, sir. Come right in, and I'll have some ice water brought right up."

The man gestured, and the gate began to open.

"Can my friend," gesturing toward his dog, "come in, too?" the traveler asked.

"I'm sorry, sir, but we don't accept pets."

The man thought a moment and then turned back toward the road and continued the way he had been going with his dog.

After another long walk, and at the top of another long hill, he came to a dirt road leading through a farm gate that looked as if it had never been closed.  There was no fence.

As he approached the gate, he saw a man inside, leaning against a tree and reading a book.

"Excuse me!" he called to the man.  "Do you have any water?"  "Yeah, sure, there's a pump over there, come on in."  "How about my friend here?" the traveler gestured to the dog.  "There should be a bowl by the pump."

They went through the gate, and sure enough, there was an old-fashioned hand pump with a bowl beside it.

The traveler filled the water bowl and took a long drink himself, then he gave some to the dog.

When they were full, he and the dog walked back toward the man who was standing by the tree.

"What do you call this place?" the traveler asked.

"This is Heaven," he answered.

"Well, that's confusing," the traveler said.  "The man down the road said that was Heaven, too."

"Oh, you mean the place with the gold street and pearly gates?  Nope.  That's hell."

"Doesn't it make you mad for them to use your name like that?"

"No, we're just happy that they screen out the folks who would leave their best friends behind."

Unknown

"Dogs feel very strongly that they should always go with you in the car, in case the need should arise for them to bark violently at nothing right in your ear."

Dave Barry

## About the Poet

It would be impossible to write a book about our kennel without including the poetic works by my Grandmother, Marie Lundgren, the first kennel attendant.

When the kennel was built in 1963, my mother and stepfather were still trying to make a living running a small dry cleaner, as well as showing and breeding dogs. The kennel was built in a then rural area, so it was a case of: "Build It And They Will Come". Fortunately for all involved, including the third generation (our son), they did.

Williamsburg now sits in the middle of one of the fastest growing areas in St. Louis County, on a six-lane highway, houses more than 240 dogs and 50 cats, and has become a true landmark in the area.

Because they were gone every weekend at dog shows, Kramer's had my Grandmother stay at the then 50 dog kennel to keep it going. As it is imperative to have someone live on the premises, she opened the office, cared for the dogs with the few employees they could afford, and obviously learned to love each and every one of the boarders.

Her poems that I've chosen to include are about her days in the kennel, but also about some personal pets that lived there. Her Doberman, Storm, was the source of many poems. Storm was truly a character, and deserves the tribute, as does my Grandmother.

**The Kennel Keeper**
**(By Marie Lundgren)**

Let Packy in, let Rosie out,
Let Spanky make a pile;
Sweep up the hair in Aaron's pen,
Hug Sadie for a while.

Let Rosie in, let Nola out,
Go get the Pooper Scooper,
And shovel here and shovel there,
We have a Champion Pooper!

So now to bring the pans of food,
A few I have to coax,
(Attention's all they really want,
'Tis just a canine hoax.)

Guy is chewing up his bed,
Storm is primed for slaughter;
The only dog he's chummy with
Is someone else's daughter.

Lexie sits within her box
That's filled with fragrant cedar;
She gazes 'round in high disdain,
For she's the Social Leader.

She's very old and very fat
And longs for veneration,
She disapproves the antics of
The present generation.

Domino is next to her
And tilts his water pan,
But Lexi turns her back on this
Uncouth and noisy man.

A cocker and a St. Bernard
Are in a pen together,
The Saint is young, the Cocker old,
But dainty as a feather.

The Saint is full of youthful glee,
Rollicking and bouncing,
But Old One makes her toe the mark
Or she will get a trouncing.

I learn their personalities,
I call them all by name;
Though some of them may look alike
No two are quite the same

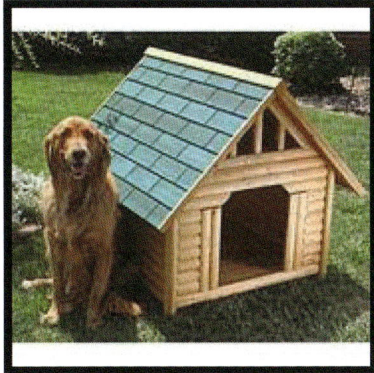

**Behind the Kennel Door**
**( By Marie Lundgren)**

I've heard since I was the age of two
Of intelligent things that canines do.
After years of seeing dogs first hand
They're the silliest creatures in all the land!

We have an exponent of Man's Best Friend,
A Rottweiler gorgeous from end to end
Who mangled the hand that stroked and fed,
Mangled the master who shared his bed.

This incident, though, I'm happy to say
Is not one that's happening everyday.
Most are just silly or playful or dumb,
Afraid of the kennel and don't want to come.

The dogs in their pens in demonic glee
Welcome the newcomer, a He or a She,
With snarling and growling and gnashing of teeth,
A show of bravado, there's nothing beneath.

The newcomer quails at the terrible din,
Tomorrow he'll snarl at the next to come in.
We have a young Boxer who gaily goes out
But bringing him in is a job for a scout.

A Weimer we're boarding is really a love,
But he'll never go out unless given a shove.
Others will cower outside of their door,
The minute it's opened they'll poop on the floor!

The piddling contests are on day and night,
All males are entered; it's a man's own birthright.
Stevie can piddle three feet and an inch,
And Storm and old Gus can make four in a pinch.

The little dogs grumble and head for the shore
While the big ones drink water to generate more.
Most of them welcome the chow and are eager,
Some are persnickety, appetites meager.

Betsy the Yorkie, a quaint little gnome,
Minces and says "I eat chicken at home."
The owners bring pillows and blankets for Missy,
Her neighbors in jealousy call her a Sissy.

A lapdog sometimes brings a basket of wicker
Which causes the others to giggle and snicker;
Poodles with hair bows are just a cut higher,
Best keep those bows away from the wire!

Often the mutts with no pedigrees bold
Are nicer than champions with collars of gold.
And here they are treated as one and the same,
Any difference between them lies only in name.

They're lovable, ornery, nutty, and yet
Each one is darling, and somebody's Pet.

# Ears and No Ears

By: Storm Von Vulcan
& Marie Burgess-Lundgren

A Doberman's life is a wonderful life,
I haven't a care in the world!
I'm glad I'm not one of those fancy dogs
That has to be barbered and curled.

I guess I was crowing a little too soon,
I guess I was getting too gay;
They took me to visit the doctor last night
And my ears have been missing all day!

I wonder if this fellow knows where they are?
I wish I could make him wake up!
He might let me borrow a bit of his ear,
He has plenty for one other pup.

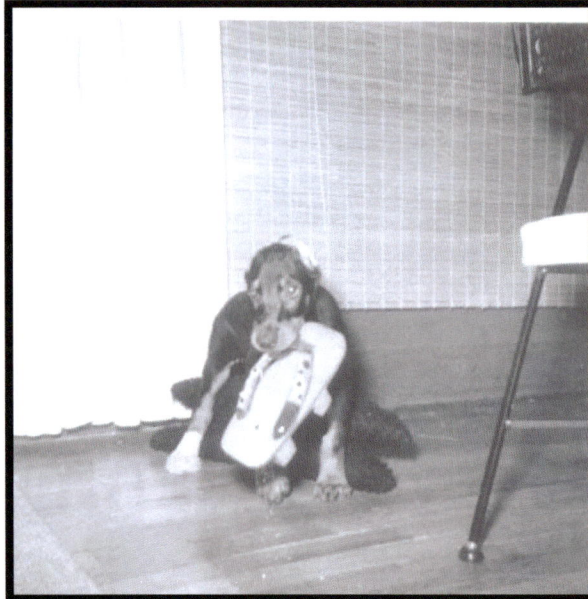

Now here is a shoe that the Japanese wear,
I wonder who left it in here?
(It's silver and blue and it's lovely to chew
But I'd trade it for one little ear!)

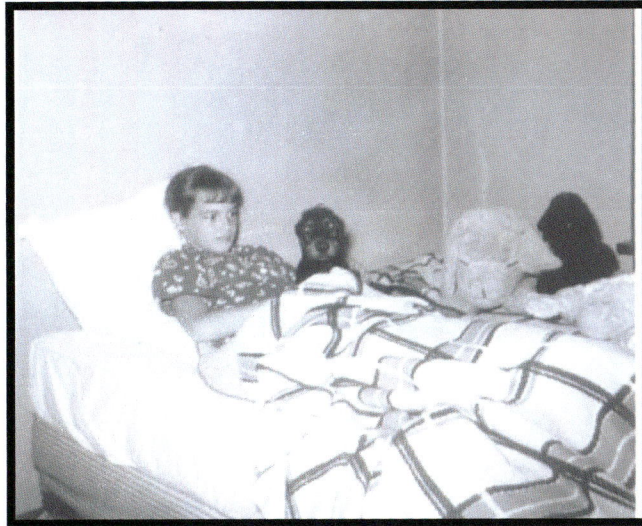

I woke up this morning and what do you think?
Back to the doctor I traveled;
And there were my ears, on the top of my head!
The mystery at last is unraveled.

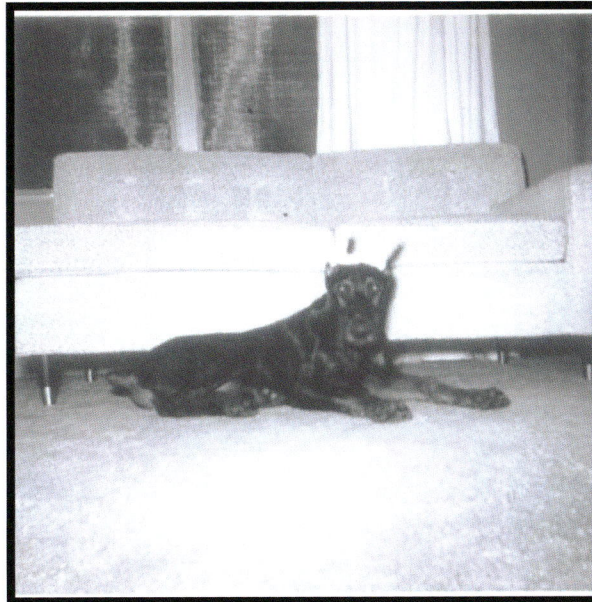

I'm to be in the show and I want you to know
We Dobes wear our ears up like this;
My Pop is a Champ and he's boss of the camp
And I mean to win trophies like his.

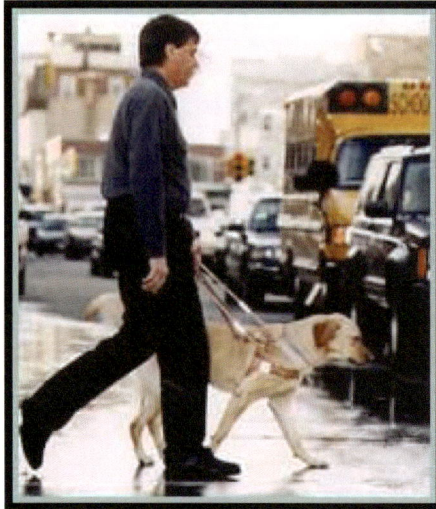

### The Seeing Eye Dog
### (By Marie Lundgren)

She led her master on the bus,
Secured for him a seat,
Then settled down upon the floor,
Her paws across his feet.

She kept an eye upon the crowd
And would not deign to sleep,
Her sense of duty toward the man
Was real, and true, and deep.

I wondered if she missed the fun
That other dogs enjoy,
Chasing rabbits in the field
Or chasing just a boy.

Or walking on the scented grass
Instead of hard concrete,
Watching kids at play, not cars
Upon a busy street.

The man reached down to stroke her head,
She kissed the kindly hand,
And I could sense the bond that just
A dog would understand.

She didn't miss the idle days
That other dogs enjoy,
Content was she to guide and be
The eyes of this, her boy.

**Dr. John Arthur & Barry**


**Veterinarian Appointment**
**(By Marie Lundgren)**

We beat a path to him for all our ills,
He gives us shots and medicine and pills.

He crops our ears and mends our broken bones,
Or docks our tails in spite of canine groans.

Sometimes he puts a pet to sleep, that's true,
Sometimes it's just the kindest thing to do.

The Doctor has a sure and gentle touch.
My appointments do not scare me very much.

But I have friends who'd rather have a bath
Than walk the Veterinarian's well-worn path.

And some of them will drag their tails
When all he's going to do is trim their nails.

Only one thing bothers me, and that's
When Doctor's waiting room is full of CATS!

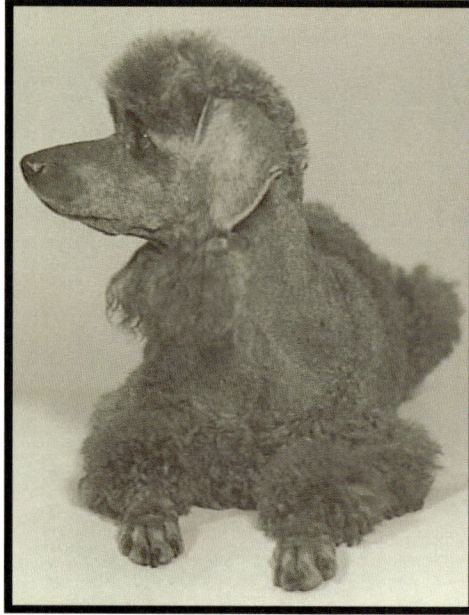

**Tou Tou Pierre**

I used to think Poodles were silly
With pom-poms and bows in their hair;
But I have revised my opinion
Since the advent of Tou Tou Pierre.

His leashes are studded with brilliants,
His coat is a barber's despair;
His pedigree papers are faultless,
His meals are selected with care.

In spite of all this he's aggressive,
And the day that I mumbled a prayer
Was the day that a Doberman Pinscher
Came charging at Tou Tou Pierre.

The scented and barbered young dandy
Stood firmly to meet the attack;
He snarled and he barked in falsetto
'Till the Dobe was jerked hurriedly back.

I don't underestimate Poodles,
I know they have hardships to bear;
And for thoughts that I had in the past
I apologize, Tou Tou Pierre!

**Storm Unabated**

**By: Storm Von Vulcan
& Marie Burgess-Lundgren**

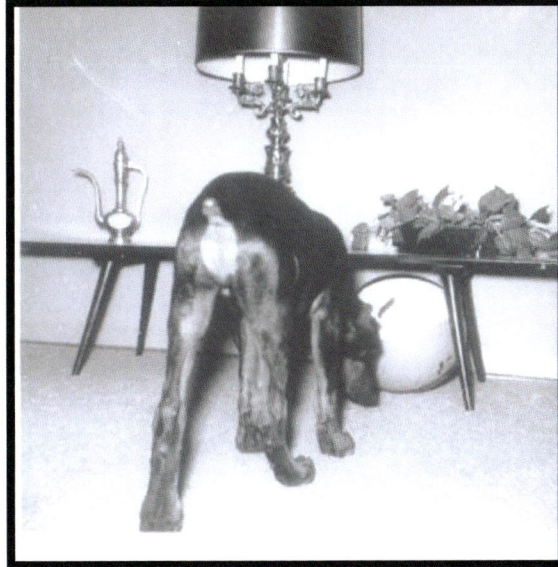

They say I am nosey, (the Family, I mean)
How else is a fellow to learn?
The world is so filled with such curious things
No matter which way I turn.

This overnight bag is a bother to me,
I dare not indulge in my passion
For teething on brushes and slippers and such,
Must behave in a dignified fashion.

This is the place where they cook all the chow,
There's something back there in a kettle;
If no one was home I could sample, perchance,
I'm hungry as Hansel and Gretel.

Maybe a drink will suffice until dinner-
Oh, darn it!  The lid's down again;
They have no respect for a poor thirsty pup,
These beings called Ladies and Men.

They let me outdoors and here's water to spare,
Enough for a year and a day;
I don't even mind when the People get in it,
I guess even folks have to play.

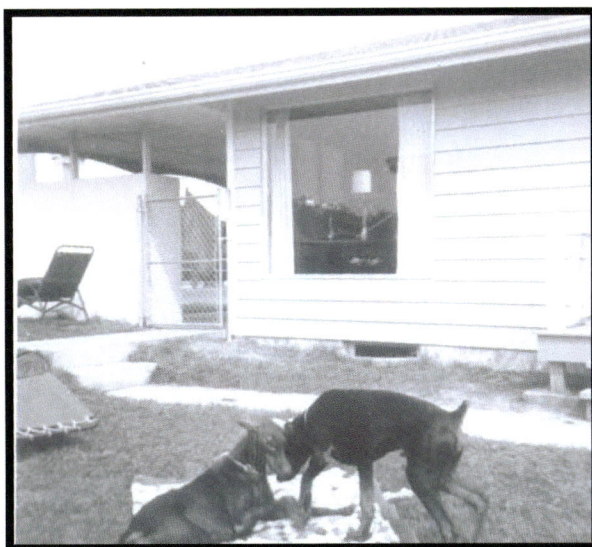

And here's my pal Damen, she's taking the sun,
Perhaps I can stir up a chase;
She's older than I but she's still rather spry,
So I always let her win the race.

### Why Do Pups?
### (By Marie Lundgren)


I bought you many pretty toys,
You silly little pup,
Rubber bones and balls with bells
And said "Go chew them up!"

You rolled them 'round and nipped a bit
In desultory play,
And when I saw you thus employed
I softly stole away.

I shopped a little, spoke with friends,
I gave you little thought
For you were with the toys
So thoughtfully I'd bought.

Why then the litter that I found
When I came in the door?
And why the tassels off my robe
In shreds upon the floor?

The bones and balls were lying there
Still shiny reds and blues
Among the flagrant debris of
My most expensive shoes!

I thought at first I'd punish you,
Alas and Oh! Alack!
I couldn't, for you kissed my hand
And said "I'm glad you're back!"

Printed in the United States
131744LV00005B